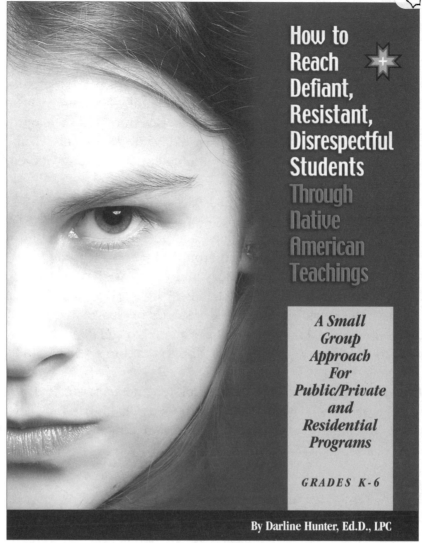

How to Reach Defiant, Resistant, Disrespectful Students Through Native American Teachings

A Small Group Approach For Public/Private and Residential Programs

GRADES K-6

By Darline Hunter, Ed.D., LPC

youth light
inc.

© 2007 by
YouthLight, Inc.
Chapin, SC 29036

Cover Design and Layout by Diane Florence
Project Editing by Susan Bowman

ISBN: 1-59850-016-3
EAN: 978-1-59850-016-5

Library of Congress Number
2006936022

10 9 8 7 6 5 4 3 2 1
Printed in the United States

Dedication

Having grown up the first child of two schoolteachers, books were my constant companions. Whether in the written or spoken word, stories were my parents' method of teaching me about the world and about myself. Nature, science, geography, literature, psychology, sociology, anthropology, and spirituality flowed through the stories they told or read to me. When my mother would tuck me into bed at night, she would recite poetry or tell me stories of the Native Americans who used to live in the surrounding country where we then lived.

So it is no wonder that I, now, gravitate toward the use of stories in my work. Whether it is as counselor, consultant, or counselor-educator, I tell stories. I tell stories to teach children how to connect with others, how to understand and accept themselves, and how to understand the strange, difficult and wonderful world around them. It is through the use of stories that our ancestors passed on their culture, history, and values. We have, I think, forgotten that lost art of story telling. I am an advocate of story telling. I am an advocate of children. Put the two together and we have this book. This is a book of stories of Native Americans and related exercises to use in the counseling of children who have a need to feel connected, to develop confidence in themselves, to learn how to be generous, and to develop a sense of independence.

My mother, who also was an advocate of children and an advocate of story telling, told many of these stories to me when I was a child. This book is a tribute to the Native American culture, my mother, and our common interest in the education and counseling of children.

Acknowledgements

I wish to acknowledge the work of Alfred Adler and Rudolf Dreikurs (Dreikurs & Soltz, 1968) who introduced me, in my Master's Degree program at the University of San Diego, to the concept that "A misbehaving child is a discouraged child." It was then the work of Brendtro, Brokenleg, and Van Bockern (1990) who were able to blend that basic Adlerian theory with the Native American culture and wisdom which I had grown up loving and believing. I am appreciative of the work of the following University of Houston Clear Lake Counseling Program students who helped to create some of the exercises in this book: Jennifer Barker-McCaffrey, Patricia Concha, Dawn Coryat, Monica McCollum, Charlotte Pyle, Candace Sexton, Rachel Sheffield, Amber Young, and Barbara Blake, a seasoned school counselor. I am especially grateful for the consultation with Shannon Sanderson, Ph.D. who fine-tuned the developmental levels for each exercise. Finally, I acknowledge the thousands of resistant, defiant, oppositional children and adolescents with whom I have been given the opportunity to interact through the public schools, agencies, hospitals, and private practice. They have given me the opportunity to truly experience what I believe life is all about......... helping one another.

Table of Contents

✳ Table of Contents

Background Information

The sense of separateness and disconnection from society and from themselves, which many children feel, is displayed in academic and legal difficulties, acting out behavior and emotional disturbance. The Native American tradition values and works to maintain harmony and balance of mind, body, and spirit with the natural environment (Reyhner, 1992; Hirschfelder & Kreipe de Montano, 1993; Deloria, 1994; Oswalt & Neely, 1999;). Experiencing this harmony through group work can facilitate a healing of the disconnectedness that children feel and are acting out. The interrelatedness of this Native American philosophy can be used to help students reconnect to society, to themselves and to nature. A review of the literature of culturally diverse group work emphasizes the blending of content, process skills and exercises to promote trust, cohesiveness and in-depth feedback, as well as individual work toward self-assigned goals (Brinson & Lee, 1997; Gladding, 1999; Haley-Banez & Walden, 1999; Furr, 2000). The healing power of nature has long been attested to by poets and prophets, but it is more currently being reviewed in the literature of counseling under the various nomenclatures of animal facilitated therapy, horticulture therapy and natural environment therapy (Crompton & Sellar, 1981; Fogle, 1981; Beck & Katcher, 1984; Bryant, 1986; Davis, 1986; Cusack, 1987; Kaplan, 1992). Religious and cultural studies indicate that humans and nature have always had a natural relationship, which provides for the spiritual and practical needs of people. Native American lore abounds with reference to and reverence for this special bond between people and nature. Contemporary writers assert that mental health may be directly related to this relationship. Just as our society has become increasingly urban, crowded, and devoid of contact with nature, so has the physical and mental health of the inhabitants of the city declined.

The further our society has moved away from contact with nature, the more distant we have become from meaningful interactions within the family, schools, and each other. Profound positive effects have been observed on participants in environmental education, school camping, and wilderness camping experiences. Increased self-esteem, self-confidence, self-concept and pride are among some of the effects of interactions with nature, as well as increased levels of responsibility and development of physical skills. Kellert and Wilson (1993) state, "This propo-

5

sition suggests that human identity and personal fulfillment somehow depend on our relationship to nature. The human need for nature is linked not just to the material exploitation of the environment but also to the influence of the natural world on our emotional, cognitive, aesthetic, and even spiritual development…" (p. 42-43). Nebbe (1995) expands on the use of Nature Therapy in the areas of instrumental therapy, relationship therapy, passive therapy, cognitive therapy and spiritual therapy. This article draws from the philosophy and activities of the Native American tradition to blend with group counseling, pet therapy and nature therapy techniques to address the needs of American school students who are suffering from a sense of disconnection from their families, schools, peers and selves.

The need for social connection is deeply rooted. The need for social inclusiveness is a deep-seated part of what it means to be human. Eisenberger and Lieberman (2004) suggest that the need to be accepted as part of a social group is an innate quality and that avoiding the emotional pain of separation is as important to humans as avoiding other types of physical pain. Being rejected by others causes distress in the pain center of the brain, the Anterior Cingulate Cortex (ACC), which registers both physical and emotional pain. The studies of Eisenberger and Lieberman (2004) suggest that social exclusion of any sort, such as abandonment, exclusion in social activities, discrimination, separation from family or friends, being lost geographically, would cause distress in the ACC. These current neurophysiological findings echo the ancient wisdom of the Native American culture.

The essence of Native American spirituality is about connection. The feeling of connection is available to all beings and experienced in a variety of ways. In the Native American Circle of Life, all things are connected; all things have purpose; and all things are worthy of respect and reverence. The circle symbolizes the cyclical nature of the world, as evidenced in the cycle of seasons and the rhythms of the sun and moon. The Medicine Wheel symbolizes the cyclical nature of the world and of the self. All four basic directions, each representing an aspect of life, are necessary for a harmonious and functional way of life. In the Cherokee teachings, the north represents the mind; the south represents the natural environment; the east represents the spirit; and the west represents the body. All aspects of life must be in balance and in harmony. In this Native American philosophy, the whole is always greater than the sum of its parts and everything in our natural environment coexists harmoniously.

Likewise, the inner dimensions of mind, body, and heart are not separate parts, but connected dimensions flowing from one another. Since this interrelationship may be disrupted by discord, the challenge is to avoid conflict, in order to balance this interrelationship of mind, body, and heart as a unified whole. All things have an important and necessary purpose in the grand scheme. Relationships are primary to the Native American philosophy and are highly influential on individual growth. Axelson (1999) translates this philosophy into the following cultural values. Individuals' behaviors are expected to be in harmony with nature. The person is valued above and beyond his/her possessions. Child rearing emphasizes self-sufficiency, which is always in harmony with nature and respect for the elderly is absolute. This ancient wisdom provides a way of thinking and behaving, which facilitates the connection of the individual to him/herself, others, his/her community, nature, and a great universal spirit. All of these points of connection aid the person in surviving and thriving physically, emotionally and spiritually in a hostile environment, whether ancient or current.

Children of today often feel disconnected from themselves, their family, their peers, the school system, and society. They often have no sense of their "place" in society and feel lost, not only geographically but, also, emotionally. In order to reach these disconnected children, counselors can use the group process to help them develop a sense of oneness with all beings. The wisdom of the Native American tradition can form a structure within which group trust and cohesiveness can heal the alienation that keeps children on the edge of society and prevents them from a fully functional and productive life. This felt sense of connection within the group process can help children bridge the differences which divide them from others and society outside the group, whether those differences are based on culture, language, or disability. The challenge for group counselors is to find ways to reach these "unreachable" youth, by building confidence, self-esteem and empathy. The values of giving, sharing and cooperation, at the core of the Native American spirituality, can open many of the closed doors of the lives of alienated children. Doors closed by language, discrimination, or disability, can be opened by teaching children that they are naturally an important part of the interconnection of all beings.

Brokenleg (1996) and Brendtro, Brokenleg, and Van Bockern (1998) proposed that when the four basic needs of all humans (belonging, mastery, independence, and generosity) are not met by the family, community, and other cultural institutions, children become alienated and act out their sense of disconnectedness. They suggest that the unmet needs of belonging can be corrected through relationships of trust and intimacy. The unmet needs of mastery can be healed through involvement in a setting with opportunities for meaningful achievement. The unmet needs of independence can be addressed with opportunities to develop positive leadership and self-discipline skills and confidence. The unmet needs of generosity can be provided through experiencing the joy of helping others. These experiences can be provided within the group counseling relationship and experience. Cullinan (2002) advocates that the schools begin to use practices that follow a philosophical direction, which will meet these basic needs. One such educational model, which is designed to address the unmet needs of belonging, mastery, independence and generosity, is proposed by Brendtro and Van Bockern (1998). Their counseling model drew upon Native American child raising philosophy to create the theme for their circle of courage model, which works to reclaim the children. It is the use, within the group setting, of the Native American philosophy of harmony and interconnectedness, blended with pet and nature therapy, which can teach students to connect with others and with themselves. Connected students feel more secure and tend to see the lesson in problems. They survive crises better and are less likely to see themselves as victims. They see the meaning in life, are more giving, and tend to think outside themselves. These connected children access and express their feelings more easily; therefore, they act out less. With improved self-esteem, they move between cultures more easily, feel and act more calmly, and are more accepting of others.

There is growing literature on the therapeutic use of the human-animal bond in education, psychology and counseling (Blue, 1986; Bryant, 1986; Melson & Peet, 1988; Ascione, 1992; Paul, 1992). Kaufman (1999) states, "With the appropriate preparation and supervision, the opportunity to play with and care for animals can provide even the most relationship-resistant youth in our schools and facilities with what they most need: a sense of connection or creature comfort." Nature has long been acknowledged as a source of healing, whether by the great spiritual traditions or by modern day psychiatric and medical facilities.

Garrett and Crutchfield (1997) developed a unity model of group work, which is a synthesis of contemporary counseling techniques and traditional Native American wisdom. Theirs is a comprehensive approach to developing self-esteem, self-determination, body awareness, and self-concept. Useful with all children, regardless of race or ethnicity, it emphasizes the universal characteristics of the need to feel a sense of belonging, mastery, independence and generosity. The focus of this article builds upon the unity model of Garrett and Crutchfield (1997) with the additional components of pet and nature therapy. This model is compatible with the Native American concepts of the harmonious coexistence of everything in our natural environment. The inner dimensions of mind, body, and spirit are not separate parts, but connected dimensions flowing from one another, whose interrelation may be disrupted by dissonance or discord.

From a Native perspective, the main purpose of such healing ceremonies is to "keep oneself in good relations," which can mean a number of things. This can mean honoring or healing a connection with oneself, between oneself and others (relationships: i.e., family, friends, and community), between oneself and the natural environment, or between oneself and the spirit world. Sometimes, healing ceremonies involve all of these. (Garrett, Garrett, & Brotherton, 2001)

It is from such healing ceremonies that the group exercises are drawn. Relationships and their influence on individual growth are accentuated. The cyclical nature of the world and self depend on harmony and balance. The four directions of the Medicine Wheel depict this harmony: the east stands for self-esteem (how one feels about self and the ability to grow and change; the south stands for self-determination (the ability to use one's own will to explore and develop potential); the west stands for body-awareness (the experience of one's physical self); the north stands for self-concept (what one thinks about oneself and one's own potential). Likewise, the Medicine Wheel can be used to depict the four components of mind, body, spirit and natural environment.

CHAPTER 1
The Need for Belonging

✵ Introduction

When the need for belonging is met, children become cooperative, friendly, affectionate, respectful, trusting and sympathetic. The group counselor can assist in the development of a positive attachment through the use of group activities, which incorporate Native American activities and philosophies. The Talking Circle is a reminder of the interrelationships with one another and with the world. "Coming together" can develop respect and acceptance of self and others. The purposes of the Talking Circle are to bring people together in a respectful manner for sharing and for teaching to occur through listening and learning. All who are within the circle have an opportunity to talk with equal respect and no interruption. A member of the Talking Circle is not expected to talk unless he/she wants to do so. Those who choose to talk are encouraged to talk, not only from the mind, but also from the heart, sharing innermost feelings. When all have spoken, the circle is closed with the reminder that all that is said in the Talking Circle is to remain within the circle and that identities and words are confidential. In this traditional way, there is a coming together to connect with each other and all living things in order to find strength and live harmoniously.

The Native American philosophy of being one with all beings ties in easily with the use of pet therapy, which assists the child to form strong emotional bonds and to develop empathy. Through interaction with animals, children learn to understand not only the feelings and needs of animals but also the feelings and needs of fellow human beings. Multiple studies (Beck & Katcher, 1984; Bryant, 1985; Blue, 1986; Bryant, 1986) have found that children owning pets felt more empathy toward other people and that animal-based education relates to higher empathy scores. Melson stated "Experiences of interconnectedness with animals and with nature may be an important context within which more nurturing children may grow to be more nurturing adults" (1990, p. 15). Interacting with animals gives children the

CHAPTER 1
The Need for Belonging

(continued)

opportunity to learn to give and receive affection, while pets substitute for human attachment by reducing loneliness, and providing love. Students deprived of positive, nurturing human affection and attachment can reduce loneliness by substituting the unconditional love given to and received from a pet (Cusack, 1987). The group counselor can point out how we are all one with nature and that we all belong to Mother Earth, noting that each member of the group breathes the same air that the animals breathe and that the same air touches each element of nature. Taking care of animals within the group setting provides opportunities for the children to consider the needs of the animals and to feel the inner satisfaction of giving of themselves as they provide for the needs of the animals. The children can project their own feelings on to the animals, which facilitates expression of feelings. The unconditional acceptance by an animal and love of the animals for the children promotes a strong sense of worth, lovability, connection and belonging.

Elder Intrigue

> ## "A chief must not seek profit for himself"
> — Sweet Medicine (Cheyenne)

Grades: 1-3

Purposes: • To provide students with opportunity to feel a connection to the past
• To provide students with opportunity to gain a respect for the elderly

Materials: • *Seya's Song* by Ron Hirschi (ISBN 0-912365-62-5)
• 3 or 4 grandparents or elders in the community willing to come in and share stories about events they have lived through or extraordinary places they have been.
• Map Colors
• Paper
• Pencils
• Comic Strip Blueprint
• Invitations

Procedures: • Day before speakers arrive, read *Seya's Song*.
(A young Sklallam girl watches baby salmon and berries ripen, gathers grass for making baskets, plays on the beach, and hikes in the mountains. Along the way her grandmother, Seya, shares the old ways and tales of past times.)
• Find Elder guests to speak to group and answer student questions.
• Students write invitations to the elders.
• Have students write thank you letters to each of the speakers.

Extensions: • Have students make comic strip drawings of their favorite story told by the elders with map colors and pencils.
• Comic strips are displayed around the room.

You Are Invited...

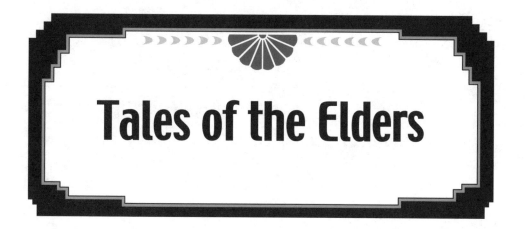

Tales of the Elders

 **Activity #2: BELONGING**

Nature Walk

"The old Lakota was wise... He knew that man's heart away from nature becomes hard"

— Luther Standing Bear

Grades: K-3

Purposes:
- To provide opportunity to experience the wonders of nature and to feel connected with Nature
- To provide opportunity to closely observe natural surroundings.
- To illustrate that father/son relationships are similar regardless of culture.

Materials:
- *Country Road* by Daniel San Souci (ISBN 0385308671)
- Someone's yard or the school playground
- What Do You See Checklist
- Paper & Pencil
- Crayons without paper wrappers
- Clipboard or something hard on which to write
- Plastic bag
- My Senses in Nature Checklist

Procedures:
- Read *Country Road.*
- Discuss:
  - Where did the boy and his Dad go for a walk?
  - What did they see on their walk in the country?
  - What memories of his Dad did the boy learn?
  - What about nature holds memories for you?
  - The Native Americans loved nature and found many memories when they walked through the woods, just as do current day people. Sit on the ground and look very closely. What do you see?
  - Walk around the yard and name all the living things you see. (Insects, plants etc.) Check them off on your *What Do You See Check List.* For Kindergarten, Verbalize the Check List.
  - Walk around the yard and find man-made things.
  - Look for signs of the season (fall, winter, spring or summer).
  - Collect seeds, acorns, leaves, pinecones etc.
  - Complete the My Senses in Nature sheet.
  - Sit down with some paper and draw what you see.

Extensions: Use the items students picked up (leaves, acorns, and rocks) to do some rubbings using the naked crayons and paper.

What Do you See
CHECKLIST

Name_____ Date_____

Check off these things you see during your nature walk.

❏ **Leaves**

❏ **Water**

❏ **Seeds**

❏ **Feather**

❏ **Twig**

❏ **Litter**

❏ **Rock**

❏ **Grass**

❏ **Bark from a tree**

My Senses in Nature
CHECKLIST

Name_____ Date_____

Assignment:

With a partner or group gather your materials and go for a nature walk.
Stay in the area assigned to you.

- Look for signs of the season. Collect seeds, acorns, leaves, pinecones etc.
- Use your crayon and paper and make rubbings of leaves, bark, soil, etc.
- Label so you remember what they are.
- Make a list in the chart below.

Things I see	Things I hear	Things I smell

- How many things were natural (part of nature)? ☐
- How many things were man-made? ☐

16

When The Storm God Rides

> *"What is life? It is the flash of a firefly in the night.*
> *It is the breath of a buffalo in the wintertime.*
> *It is the little shadow which runs across the grass and loses*
> *itself in the sunset."*
>
> — Crowfoot, Blackfoot Warrior and Orator

Grades: K-2

Purposes:
- To create a sense of belonging and connection with Nature
- To provide opportunity to express themselves musically
- To provide opportunity to simulate or mimic sounds heard in Nature
- To teach that each individual is important to the whole

Materials:
- *When the Storm God Rides* by Florence Stratton
- Sound machine that has thunderstorm feature
- Pens
- Desk
- Windows or something made of glass
- Books (hardbacks)
- Washboard and wood stick (optional)
- 2 Flash Lights
- Spoon
- Paper
- Aluminum foil
- 1 pair of shoes with hard heals

Procedures:
- Read "When the Storm God Rides."
- Talk about how before the rain there is silence, then it starts off softly and grows louder gradually, then as it dies down it gradually gets softer.
- Listen to sound machine's thunderstorm.
- Ask the students what individual sounds they heard.
- Give students a storm function (rain, thunder, or lightning).
- Explain what tools mimic which sound.
- <u>Rain</u> - Rubbing hands together, pouring water from one glass into another, pencils tapping on a desk or book, pencils or spoon tapping on glass or window, flicking tongue against roof of mouth, stomping feet lightly on ground, clicking heels against tile floor, and shaking aluminum foil.
- <u>Thunder</u> - Dropping hardback book on tile or carpet, slamming book closed, rubbing washboard with wooden stick, and clapping hands together
- <u>Lightning</u> - Turning flashlight on & off, crackling paper into ball, and flipping light switch off and on or if you have access to music room instruments, you can use a wind chime or triangle.
- Then add rain sticks. Then add maracas, and tambourines. Then add thunder with cymbals, then some drums. After this, let the storm get very loud.
- Then take away the drums and cymbals. Then take away the maracas and tambourines. All that is left playing now is rain sticks and the wind chime or triangle. Finally take out the rain sticks. All that is playing is the wind chime or triangle. Take that away and then silence.
- They have just created their very own rainstorm! The kids will want to do this over and over again.

Extensions:
- Can repeat the process, but this time have posters with the words DRIZZLE, SPRINKLE, SHOWER, HARD RAIN, MILD THUNDER STORM, HEAVY THUNDER STORM.
- Hold up the signs and tell the students to change the way they make their individual sounds based on the sign being held up.
- Point out that there are as many kinds of rainstorms as there are kinds of people. All are important to Nature.
- Discuss how different intensity of behavior is appropriate at different times. For instance a giggle in class or church is appropriate, where as a loud belly laugh is more appropriate for the playground.

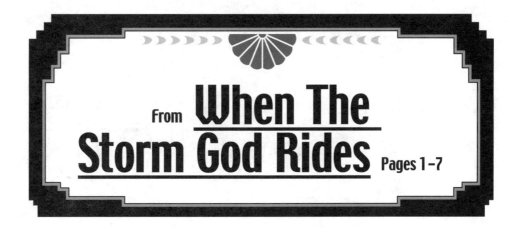

From **When The Storm God Rides** Pages 1–7

The shores of Texas along the Gulf of Mexico did not always have islands along them. The Indians who lived a long time ago on the coast have left behind them the story of a god and his great black-winged thunderbird, which he rode like a horse over the Gulf at certain times. He was the Storm God, and he made islands where none had been before. These islands were made as homes for the wild birds, the sea gulls, the big pelicans, the cranes and the herons.

The god of storms did not live among the Indians, but lived down in the warm seas below the Gulf of Mexico. And for this the Indians were glad, for his terrible thunderbird, named Hurakan, filled the people with fear. The tribes, which lived near the Gulf, only saw the mighty god when he rode his thunderbird through the skies. He visited their land when he wanted to get the white and colored feathers of birds living on the seashore for his cloak. The Indians could tell when he was on the way. As Hurakan, the thunderbird, came swiftly through the air over the gulf, the sky in front of him became filled with bits of white clouds sailing high over the beaches. Then the wind began to bow, first here, then there. At last came the great thunderbird in the shape of a cloud, which closed the eye of the sun and made the land dark. Then the wind grew strong and howled and blew as the god and his thunderbird came flying through the sky. The Indians ran into their wigwams and held them down as best they could while the Storm God rushed by and snatched feathers from birds to put on his cloak. The Indians were happy when he was gone because Hurakan made them afraid. Even today Hurakan comes back once in a while in the shape of a storm which people call a hurricane.

There was a day when the peaceful tribes who fished in the Gulf were driven away from their homes by fierce tribes from the north. Unlike the Indians who lived on the coast these tribes like to kill. When they saw the birds flying around, they shot them with arrows. They caught them on their roosts at night. They robbed their nests. The poor birds cried out at the tops of their voices for the Storm God to save them.

Far off down in his home in the warm seas the god lifted his head and heard their cries. Quickly he rose to his feet and shook himself. Thunder broke loose over his head, so angry was he. He ran and jumped upon the back of Hurakan. He shouted for Hurakan to hurry. Shooting fire like lightning from his eyes and shaking loose black clouds from the tips of his great wings the Storm God's thunder bird flew toward the Texas coast. He and the god were wrapped in darkness, and as they flew across the sky the day became like night and the waters of the Gulf broke into white foam.

From **When The Storm God Rides** (cont.)

The Indians who were killing the birds saw the thunder god coming too late to get away. The sun was gone and the clouds were so thick that the day was like night. The wind from Hurakan's wings hit the Indians and blew them down when they tried to run. Behind them came the waters of the Gulf, pushed upon the land by the wind stirred up by the Storm God's thunderbird. The wind blew the birds high in the air, but it drove the water into the camps of the bad Indians and scattered their homes and made the Indians climb into trees. The Gulf now poured far inland over the prairie, and the prairie was like the sea. Everywhere was rolling water, leaping waves, crying winds. High above the earth the Storm God rode his thunderbird and shouted with joy while the wind blew his long hair loose through the flying clouds.

At last the god went away. As he left, the waters of the Gulf began to roll back from the land, and when they reached the ocean bed again they dropped the mud and sand they had torn loose from the land and brought with them. The mud and sand began to pile up. Soon many islands were forming. They rose higher and higher as the waters kept dropping their loads of earth around them. When all was done the Texas coast was dotted with islands that were new homes for the birds. Indians could not reach those birds any longer. The pelicans, the gulls, the sand pipers and all the others now went to their new homes and made their nests where they could be safe and where the Storm God could find them when he wanted new feathers for his cloak.

To this day those islands remain. Dwarf trees, cactus plants, weeds, grasses and flowers cover them like fairy gardens. And thousands of birds live on them, sing amid the bushes and bathe in the little pools left by the rains. During spring and summer they lay their eggs and raise their little ones. They are happy and safe from men, because long ago the Storm God built the islands for them.

 **Activity #4: BELONGING**

Forgiveness Strawberries

> *"I have seen that in any great undertaking*
> *it is not enough for a man to depend simply upon himself."*
> — Lone Man (Isna-la-wica), Teton Sioux

Grades: K-5

Purpose: To develop appropriate ways to release feelings of anger, hurt, and forgiveness.

Materials: *The First Strawberries: A Cherokee Story* by Joseph Bruchac
(ISBN 0140564098)
Paper
Markers/crayons
Scissors
Strawberry worksheet
Strawberries

Summary: This legend explains the origins of strawberries, grown by the sun to help the first man and woman patch a quarrel. In this story, the Sun heals a quarrel by a husband and wife. The Sun gives the gift of ripe strawberries that magically grow at the feet of an angry woman while she flees her husband's harsh words, thus halting her departure long enough for him to catch up and make amends. Thereafter, the story concludes, whenever the Cherokee eat strawberries, they are reminded to be kind to one another.

Procedures: Read *The First Strawberries: A Cherokee Story*.

Discuss: What lessons did both the man and woman learn?
Encourage the children to retell the story.
Make a list of the natural resources used in the story such as the various fruits, clothing, and any others they observe in the illustrations. Discuss with the children how nature (the sun and berries) taught the people to forgive each other. Ask children how people felt about nature in this story. Have the students describe, write, or draw about a time when they have forgiven someone. Discuss or write how forgiveness makes them feel on the Forgiveness Strawberries Template. Later decorate a bulletin board with all of the Forgiveness Strawberries. Afterwards, enjoy some fresh strawberries!

Extension: Children could be given forgiveness scenarios to role-play.

Forgiveness Strawberries

Write in the strawberry what you learned from the story.
- Have you ever forgiven someone?
- Has someone ever forgiven you?
- Why is that important?

Color and cut out the strawberry.

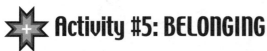

Helping the Earth

> "Every step you take should be a prayer.
> And if every step you take is a prayer,
> then you will always be walking in a sacred manner."
>
> — Oglala Lakota Holyman

Grades: K-5

Purpose: To develop a sense of belonging
To learn to cooperate
To learn to be respectful of each other and the earth

Materials: *Brother Eagle, Sister Sky: A Message from Chief Seattle* by Susan Jeffers
(ISBN 0803709692)
Poster Board
Markers
Helping the Earth Worksheet

Summary: This picture book is actually a message from Chief Seattle spoken over 100 years ago. It is a beautiful plea to help preserve and protect the land and those that live upon it. He says that the earth does not belong to us, but we belong to it, and that all things are connected in a web. He explains that what we do to parts of that web, we do to ourselves.

Procedures: Read *Brother Eagle, Sister Sky: A Message from Chief Seattle*.

Discuss: • How has the earth changed over the past 100 years since Chief Seattle made his speech?
• What ways can we help the earth?
• What would happen if every person on the earth performed one nice task every day?
• What would the world be like?

Fill in the Helping The Earth Worksheet to demonstrate how people can help each other and the earth.

Extension: • Organize a group to clean up a neighborhood or park.
• Make a *Helping The Earth* poster to display in the hall.

Helping the Earth

In the speech bubbles, write down an idea of what each person could do to help each other or the earth.

 **Activity #6: BELONGING**

Animal Tracks

> "Brothers, we must be united;
> we must smoke the same pipe; we must fight each other's battles;
> and more than all, we must love the Great Spirit."
> — Tecumseh Shawnee

Grades: K-3

Purpose: To be respectful of nature

Materials: *Reading the Wild* by Bev Doolittle (ISBN 086713061X)
Paper
Pencils
Animal Tracks Worksheet

Summary: Native Americans knew how to "read" the wild and felt privileged to learn from their wilderness relatives. Plants, trees, animals, birds, reptiles, and amphibians, all have secrets to tell; it takes only paying attention and a little knowledge and you, too, can begin to create the story that explains the disappearing snowshoe hare tracks, or how the fawn got its spots, or why Native Americans always associated the bear with healing and medicine. Notice how coyotes are clever clowns with many characteristics we think of as "human," and learn how the badger builds mansions underground with rooms for sleeping, eating, and raising their young.

Procedures:
- Read *Reading the Wild*.
- Have students go outside and look for animal tracks, insect tracks, or any sign left by one of Earth's creatures.
- Have students write their own story about the tracks.
- Allow students to write from the perspective of the animal.
- What would the animal say to us?
- Kindergarten and first grade verbalize their stories.

Extension: Have the students make their own tracks in the dirt, sand, or snow and write a story to go along with them.

Animal Tracks

_____

_____

_____

_____

_____

_____

_____

_____

_____

_____

_____

_____

_____

My Helpers

> "I have seen that in any great undertaking
> it is not enough for a man to depend
> simply upon himself."
>
> — Lone Man

Grades: 2-6

Purpose: To gain an awareness of support systems in place in our lives
To understand why and when a support system is necessary

Materials: *Return to the Land: The Search for Compassion* by Tom Carr
Drawing paper
Crayons/markers
Magazine pictures of relationships
Thank You Card Template
Thank You Letter Template

Procedures: • Read #3 Compassion For the Blind Creatures in
Return to the Land: The Search for Compassion.

Discuss:
• How was the blind rat helped by the others?
• How was Hinge, the canary, helped by Crusty, his mate?
• Students will discuss the people in magazine pictures that show different kinds of relationships – entire families, friends, neighbors, siblings, teachers.
• How do the people in the pictures depend on each other?
• How can they help each other with problem situations?

• Students name people in their lives who they can trust to help them.
• Students illustrate in drawings an event in their lives in which they have needed help from someone and show how the help was given.
• Students will share their drawings.
• Closing discussion will center around who students can go to for help with various problems.

Extension: Students can write a letter to thank the person who helped them with a specific problem in the past. Younger students make a Thank You Card to give to someone who has helped the child.

Thank You for Helping Me

Dear _____ ,

Thank you for helping me with

_____

_____

_____

_____

_____

Sincerely,

_____

Date _____

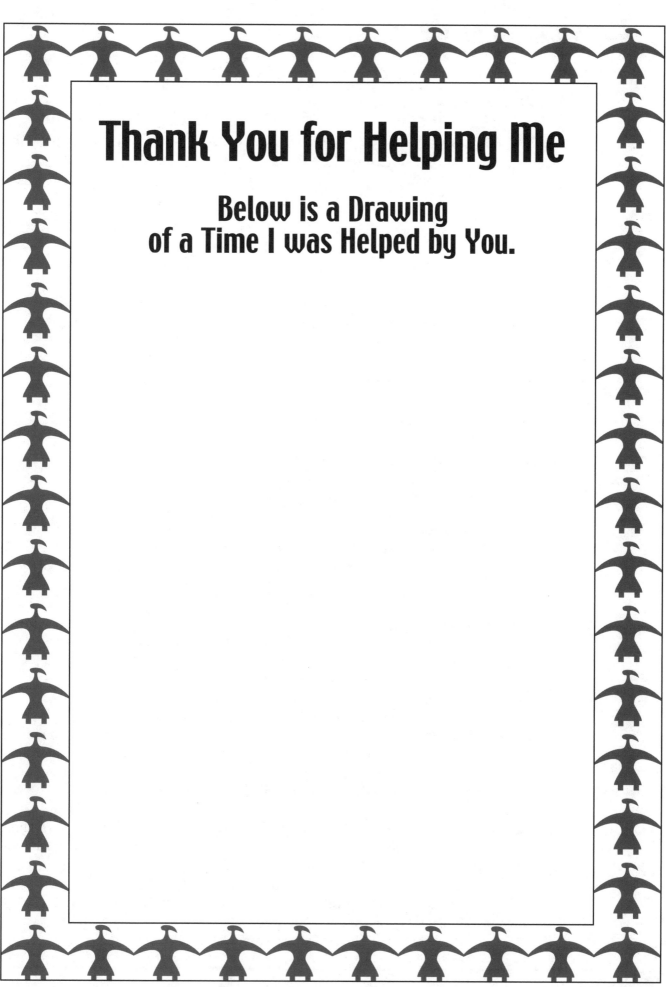

Thank You for Helping Me

Below is a Drawing
of a Time I was Helped by You.

Activity #8: BELONGING

The Diversity Within

> "There are many things to be shared with the Four Colors of humanity in our common destiny as one with our Mother the Earth. It is this sharing that must be considered with great care by the Elders and the medicine people who carry the Sacred Trusts, so that no harm may come to people through ignorance and misuse of these powerful forces."
>
> — Resolution of the Fifth Annual Meetings of the Traditional Elders Circle, 1980

Grades: K-5

Purpose: To value the diversity in one's immediate surroundings.
To recognize the differences among members of groups but still maintain interconnectedness.

Materials: *Return to the Land: The Search for Compassion* by Tom Carr
ISBN 1-889636-64-9
Music brought by students
Stereo system
We Are Different, But We Are One Worksheet

Procedures:
- Read #85 The Tale of the One-Eyed Robin in *Return to the Land: The Search for Compassion*.

  Discuss:
  - How did the mice help the Eskimos?
  - How did the Eskimos help the mice?
  - We are all different, but we are all in this life together.
  - We can help each other better because of our differences.

- Students who have been in a group together for a while and have established a strong sense of connectedness are asked to express their diversity through their choice of music and the music of their cultural heritage.
- Students bring music to play and explain any historical/cultural significance of which they are aware.
- Students take turns demonstrating a dance.
- Differences in musical tastes and styles of dance are discussed.
- Students give their own explanations for how people in a group (family, friends, etc.) can get along well with each other and have such different preferences when it comes to things like music, clothing, movies, food.
- Kindergarten and First Grade verbalize the survey.

Extension: Using the *We Are Different Worksheet* students are to take a survey of family differences and similarities. They will note if these differences interfere with the interaction of the family members. This will be reported to the group the following week. Note: Allow students to list own family members. Do not assume they come from the typical nuclear family. Students with limited writing ability may draw a picture of their family enjoying each other despite their individual differences.

We Are Different But We Are One

SURVEY

Family Members	Favorite Food	Music	TV	Hobbies
1.				
2.				
3.				
4.				
5.				
6.				
7.				

Results of Survey: List family members who agree on:

Food _____

Music _____

TV _____

Hobbies _____

Beauty of Colors

> "Make happy tracks in many snows,
> and may the rainbow always touch your shoulder."
>
> — Cherokee Prayer Blessing

Grades: K-5

Purposes:
- To provide opportunity to understand and appreciate the value of the differences in people.
- To appreciate the beauty of nature.
- To provide an opportunity to learn that helping others is a way of sharing self with others.

Materials:
"When the Rainbow Was Torn" in *When the Storm God Rides* by Florence Stratton
Water colors and brushes
Drawing paper
Rainbow Worksheet

Procedures:
• Read "When the Rainbow Was Torn."

Discuss:
- For what had the white cactus flowers hoped?
- Why was the rainbow afraid to touch the cactus flowers?
- What are some of your favorite colors which you see in Nature?

• Students are shown the picture of a rainbow and discuss the different colors seen and the awesome beauty of it that we may take for granted.
• They name other colors that they do not see in the rainbow.
• Students paint their own rainbow using the same colors in the picture.
• Younger children color in the Rainbow Worksheet
• Counselor comments on anyone who may be blending two colors, which create a third, color.

Discuss:
- When we influence and help each other, we are blending ourselves just like the colors on the paper are blending.
- Students give examples of situations where a project or event is improved when more people cooperate and help.

Extension:
Students write a poem about the colors they have seen in the rainbow and how colors blend and help each other to make new colors, just as our lives are changed and enriched by the people around us.

May The Rainbow Always Touch Your Shoulder

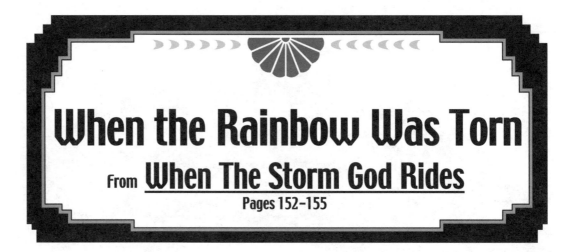

When the Rainbow Was Torn
From When The Storm God Rides
Pages 152–155

There are flowers whose petals have in them part of the very colors belonging to the rainbow. These are the cactus flowers, the blooms that burst out like orange, red or yellow flame from the tips of the thorny cactus plants. It used to be that all these flowers were white, as some are now. But one day the rainbow gave most of them colors which they have kept up to this time.

The white cactus flowers used to turn up their faces and look at the bright bow that arched across the sky whenever the sun shone through the rain or mist. The two ends of the rainbow always touched the earth somewhere, and where they touched everything on the ground seemed to be washed in the rainbow's colors. But the rainbow had never touched the cactus plants. Perhaps it was afraid of the sharp thorns that grew on them. The white cactus flowers always hoped that some day they would be bathed in misty colors. Yet the rainbow would never come near them.

Once after a heavy rain the rainbow was up in the sky getting ready to send its two ends down to earth. The rainbow itself was heavy with raindrops. As its ends sand down it took care not to let them fall upon the thorns of the cactus plants. But, just as one of the ends was about to dip to the ground the rainbow suddenly saw a bed of cactus plants hidden in a little cluster of high grass. When it saw the plants the rainbow tried to lift its end again, but the end was so heavy with the raindrops that it kept sinking down, and at last it brushed across the cactus plants with their white flowers.

When this happened the thorns caught at the misty bands of colors to try to keep them for the flowers. The violet, indigo, blue and green bands slipped out of their way, but the yellow, red and orange bands became hung on the thorns. Just as soon as this happened the happy cactus flowers opened their petals wide and began to drink in the colored mists that were clinging to the plants. Before the rainbow had pulled itself loose from the thorns the white flowers had filled themselves with the colors and were now red and orange and yellow themselves.

 **Activity #10: BELONGING**

A Quilted Family Tree

> "Everything on the earth has a purpose, every disease an herb to cure it, and every person a mission. This is the Indian theory of existence."
>
> — Morning Dove Salish

Grades: 1-6

Purpose: To recognize that each person plays an important role in his/her family and the lives of others.

Materials: *The Patchwork Quilt* by Valerie Flournoy ISBN # 0-590-89753-5
A quilt or pictures of a quilt
Quilting Sheet
Crayons/Markers
Pen/Pencil
Craft Scissors with Border Edges
Glue
Construction Paper

Procedures:
• Read *The Patchwork Quilt.*
• Show a quilt to the group or show pictures of quilts.
  Discuss: • How the Settlers made quilts from scraps of left over material.
  • Each patch has special meaning and is specially made for the quilts.
  • Families are similar.
  • Each person plays a unique role in his or her family.
  • Each of these roles is important to the functioning of the family.

• Have students complete the quilt with each patch being dedicated to a different person and how they contribute to their family. These people do not necessarily have to be blood relatives; they can be people that the members consider part of their family. Once students complete each patch, they can cut them out with the craft scissors and glue them onto construction paper making their quilted tree complete. The center patch should be the group member's patch. Allow students to show and discuss their quilts with the group.

Extension: Have the group members discuss and compare the roles they play in their families. Encourage students to journal about how they feel about the roles they play in their families. Encourage group members to journal ways in which they may choose to change the role they play in their family.

Quilted Family Tree

 **Activity #11: BELONGING**

The People of Our Lives

> "Love is something we must have.
> We must have it because our spirits feed upon it."
>
> — Chief Dan George

Grades: 4-8

Purpose: To provide an opportunity for group members to recognize people who have greatly influenced their lives and helped make them who they are.

Materials: *Return to the Land: The Search for Compassion* by Tom Carr
                      ISBN 1-889636-64-9
                  Pen/Pencil
                  Crayons, Markers, or Map Pencils
                  Roll of Honor
                  Certificate of Appreciation

Procedures: • Read #116 Animals Seeking Human Help in *Return to the Land: The Search for Compassion.*

Discuss: • How did humans help animals in this story?
                    • Who has helped you in your life?
                    • What influence can other people have in our lives?
                    • How do these relationships shape who we are?

                  • Show students a pictorial timeline. Each person on the timeline will be someone who positively affected the student's life.
                  • The students will then create their own timeline that represents different people who have influenced their lives.
                  • Students show and discuss their finished Time Lines with the group.

Extension: • Students can pick the person who influenced their life the greatest and write them a thank you letter.
                  • If possible, students can deliver the letters to the influential person.
                  • Stage an Honoring Ceremony in which the students present a token of appreciation to a person who has influenced them.
                  • Students plan the ceremony, write invitations, make tokens/certificates of appreciation and conduct the ceremony.

Roll of Honor

In each empty box draw a person who has greatly influenced your life. On the lines beside the box, write a brief description of how this person has influenced your life.

In Appreciation

For the Influence You Have Had on My Life

I Present to You,

_____

This Token of My Appreciation.

Signed _____

Date _____

 ## Activity #12: BELONGING

The Family Bundle

> "A single twig breaks,
> but the bundle of twigs is strong."
>
> — Tecumesh

Grades: 2-6

Purposes:
- To promote awareness of what qualities make families strong.
- To recognize the different types of families that exist.
- To recognize to what type of family the students belong.

Materials: *Return to the Land: The Search for Compassion* by Tom Carr
      ISBN 1-889636-64-9
    Collage Sheet
    Magazines
    Scissors
    Glue
    Tooth picks

Procedures:
- Read #110 Quail Hardships in *Return to the Land: The Search for Compassion*
  - **Discuss:**
    - How do the members of the Quail family, or covey, work together to help each other?
    - What was the job of the female quail?
    - How was the Quail family stronger together than separately?
    - How is your family stronger together than separately?
    - Each helper makes "The Family Bundle" stronger.
- Students bundle toothpicks together.
- Students break one toothpick and then to try to break their bundle.
  - **Discuss:**
    - The same concept as applied to families.
    - What qualities make families strong?
    - What defines a family?
    - What different types of families exist?
- Each student creates a collage of pictures cut out of magazines, which represent his/her family and the interests and activities of that family.

Extension:
- Give students the opportunity to share their collages with the group.
- Display the Family Bundle Collages.
- Have the students write a reflection discussing their role in their family and how their own personal qualities add to the strength of the Family Bundle.

Family Bundle Collage

 **Activity #13: BELONGING**

Bubbles

> "I do not want war at all, but want to make friends,
> and am doing the best I can for that purpose."
>
> — Santanta

Grades: 3-6

Purposes:
- To help develop recognition of the different groups to which they belong.
- To promote coping skills for managing the difficulties or conflicts that may arise as a result of feeling a sense of loyalty to various groups.

Materials: "How the North Wind Lost his Hair" from *When the Storm God Rides*
     by Florence Stratton
Pen or Pencil
Bubble Map for Groups
Small jars of bubble mixture and wands for each student

Procedures: • Read "How the North Wind Lost his Hair"
   Discuss: • Why were the North Wind and the South Wind fighting?
      • Who won the fight?
      • The two winds belonged to two different groups or parts of the country. What was positive about each group?
      • We all belong to different groups and classify ourselves based on those groups. For example: counselor, employee, woman, mother, sister, daughter.)
      • How do our roles change when we are in these different groups? (For example, I may not talk to my brothers the same as I would talk to my co-workers.)
   • Complete the bubble map listing groups to which students belong.
   • Students discuss difficulties that may occur from belonging to groups that overlap. For example I may want to spend more time with my friends when I need to do things to get prepared for work.
   • For younger students, distribute small bottles of soapy water with bubble wand. As students blow bubbles, have them call out and name the bubbles according to the various roles/groups of which they are a part.

Extension: • Have the students journal over the next week about the conflicts or positive things they may experience from belonging to a variety of groups.
   • Share in the next session.

Bubble Map

Complete the bubble map below by writing your name in the center circle and write the names of the groups you belong to in the circles that extend from the center circle. You do not have to use all of the circles.

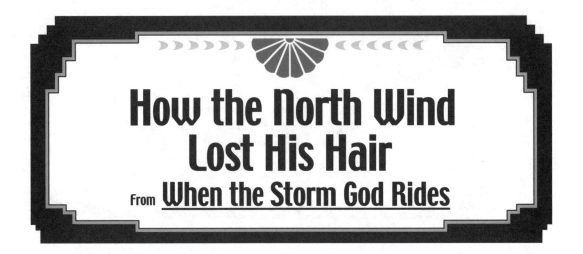

How the North Wind Lost His Hair
From When the Storm God Rides

The howling old north wind is afraid to come to the country around the Gulf of Mexico. Only now and then does this cold fellow dare to come into the south, and when he does he does not stay long. He is afraid of the strong young south wind. Once the two winds had a great fight. There are still signs of that fight in the southern woods. The Natchez and the Tejas Indians, who lived along the gulf, had a story to tell about the north and the south winds and why the moss that grows in the trees is a sign of their fight.

The two winds hated each other. The north wind was a strong, fierce old man with long, thick, gray hair. When he came into the southern woods, where the south wind lived, he would rush around blowing cold out of his mouth. His gray hair would fly behind him like a dark cloud. Nobody liked the old north wind. The Indians shivered in their tents and the flowers closed up and died when he came around. But everybody liked the warm young south wind, for he lived there. The flowers always opened up when he touched them with his soft hands and breathed upon their buds. The Indians would roam through the woods when he was with them.

From time to time the north wind and the south wind would grow angry with each other. The old north wind would come down out of his country where he belonged and try to drive the south wind away from his home along the Gulf. Sometimes he would bring his blanket of snow with him and stay for weeks. When the south wind would try to drive him out of the woods and send him home again the north wind would puff up his red cheeks and blow cold air around, and his long gray hair would fly over his head.

One spring the old north wind came south and would not go away. He stayed for many weeks after the flowers should have been coming out and the birds should have been building their nests. It was so cold the leaves would not come out on the bare limbs of the trees. June came, but still the Gulf country looked as it looked during the winter months. The north wind kept blowing the south wind out over the Gulf, and because of this the spring weather would not come.

Finally the young south wind became tired of staying over the Gulf so long. He made up his mind to gather all his power and to enter into a great fight with the north wind that had driven him from his home. Filling his lungs with all the air he could hold, the south wind rushed across

44

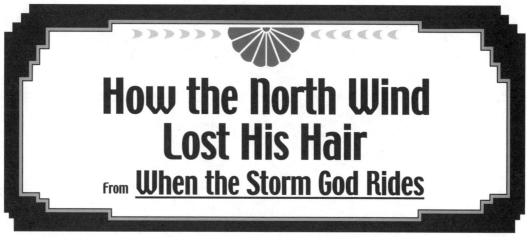

How the North Wind Lost His Hair

From **When the Storm God Rides**

(continued)

the water toward the land. He hit the north wind a mighty blow. When the two winds locked themselves in each other's arms and began howling in each other's faces the Indians ran into their tents, thinking the Storm God was riding over their heads on his thunder bird that breathed out the lightning. The fighting winds knocked around the clouds in the sky and tore them to pieces as they fought. They pulled up trees; they caused great waves to dash on the beach, they whirled birds around in the air, they tore up the snow that lay on the ground. They ran through the trees, they rolled on the earth and they clawed an shrieked.

At last the young south wind began to get the better of the old north wind. The old fellow was out of breath, and because he was out of breath he lost his power. Then the south wind wrapped his arms in the north wind's long gray hair and began whirling him round and round over his head. He whirled him faster and faster. A strange thing happened. Part of the north Wind's gray hair broke loose, and he flew howling through the air.

There stood the young south wind with his strong arms full of hair. He was so happy that he began dancing around and swinging the north wind's hair over the trees. The birds sang and the Indians shouted, for they were glad the south wind had come home again. As the south wind danced and whirled around he let the hair loose, and it fell all over the trees, and where it fell it took root. There it grew and still grows today. It is called Spanish moss. It hangs from the magnolia, oak, gum, and other trees in long gray beards that sometimes dip in the streams.

The north wind does not stay in the south any more. When he sees the moss he remembers that fight with the south wind and he leaves as fast as he can.

Activity #14: BELONGING

We Are Family

> "You have noticed that everything an Indian does is in a circle…"
> — Black Elk Oglala Sioux Holy Man

Grades: 4-8

Purposes: To make students aware of their connectedness to each other and those around them.

Materials: *Return to the Land: The Search for Compassion* by Tom Carr
ISBN 1-889636-64-9
Variety of balls of yarn in many different colors (purple, white, green, blue, yellow, orange, etc.)

Procedures:
- Read # 82 A Special Friendship: Through the Window in *Return to the Land: The Search for Compassion* by Tom Carr

  Discuss:
  - Each part of Nature is connected.
  - Who were the friends in this story?
  - Have you ever been friends with an animal or bird?

- Divide students into groups of 3-4
- Give each group a ball of yarn
- Have each group label their color of yarn with a word that represents that color (ex: red – love, black – hate)
- Everyone in each group needs to have some yarn in their hands. For example, in the group with the red yarn, each member should have some red yarn in their hands without cutting the yarn.
- When everyone in the group has yarn in their hand, then they gently toss the yarn to another group (DO NOT CUT THE YARN!)
- The yarn is then passed around to everyone in that group until everyone has that color in their hands.
- This continues until everyone in the room has every color of yarn in their hands.

  Discuss:
  - If one person pulls the yarn in his/her hands, does anyone else feel it? Why or why not?
  - What if several people drop their yarn?
  - Can anyone else feel it?
  - How are we affected if one group tries to take a color that we don't want to give up?
  - How does this relate to connectedness and belonging? Are we all connected to each other somehow?

Extension:
- Instead of yarn, cut puzzle pieces out of poster board and pass out to each student to form a big puzzle.
- Have each student decorate a puzzle piece, and place in the puzzle.
- What happens when a piece of the puzzle is missing?
- For younger students, use a ready-made puzzle and put together as a class.

North Wind – South Wind Words

> "My heart laughs with joy because I am in your presence."
> — Chitmachas Chief

Grades: 1-5

Purpose: To identify the significance of others in our lives
To increase the understanding and acceptance of others

Materials: "How the North Wind Lost His Hair" from *When The Storm God Rides*
   by Florence Stratton
Pencil
South Wind Words Worksheet

Procedures: • Read "How the North Wind Lost His Hair."
  Discuss: • How is the North Wind like someone who hurts our feelings?
     • What did he do to hurt the feelings of the Indians and flowers?
     • How is the South Wind like someone saying nice things to us?
     • What did he do to the Indians and flowers to help them?
     • Which wind was liked the best?
     • If the winds were words, what would be some North Wind words?
     • What would be some South Wind words?
     • How have your feelings been hurt in the past?
     • How may you have hurt someone else's feelings.
     • Brainstorm a list of nice things (South Wind Words) we could say to people.
• Have each student complete the You Are Special Because Worksheet.
• Everyone writes down a compliment (South Wind words) about each student.
• First Grade can verbalize the Worksheet.

Extension: • Role-play being the North Wind, then the South Wind, then the two winds fighting.
• Role-play saying nice things to each other (using South Wind words)

South Wind Words:
You Are Special Because...

Things that I like about you are...

1. _____

2. _____

I like it when you...

1. _____

2. _____

It makes me laugh when you...

1. _____

2. _____

You are my friend because...

1. _____

2. _____

48

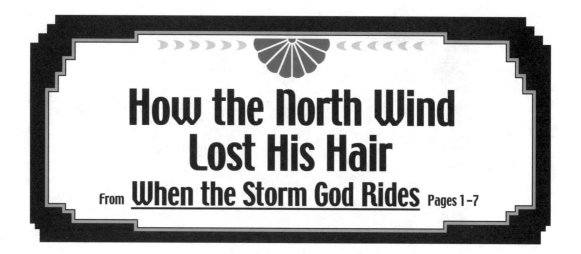

How the North Wind Lost His Hair

From <u>When the Storm God Rides</u> Pages 1–7

The howling old north wind is afraid to come to the country around the Gulf of Mexico. Only now and then does this cold fellow dare to come into the south, and when he does he does not stay long. He is afraid of the strong young south wind. Once the two winds had a great fight. There are still signs of that fight in the southern woods. The Natchez and the Tejas Indians, who lived along the gulf, had a story to tell about the north and the south winds and why the moss that grows in the trees is a sign of their fight.

The two winds hated each other. The north wind was a strong, fierce old man with long, thick, gray hair. When he came into the southern woods, where the south wind lived, he would rush around blowing cold out of his mouth. His gray hair would fly behind him like a dark cloud. Nobody liked the old north wind. The Indians shivered in their tents and the flowers closed up and died when he came around. But everybody liked the warm young south wind, for he lived there. The flowers always opened up when he touched them with his soft hands and breathed upon their buds. The Indians would roam through the woods when he was with them.

From time to time the north wind and the south wind would grow angry with each other. The old north wind would come down out of his country where he belonged and try to drive the south wind away from his home along the Gulf. Sometimes he would bring his blanket of snow with him and stay for weeks. When the south wind would try to drive him out of the woods and send him home again the north wind would puff up his red cheeks and blow cold air around, and his long gray hair would fly over his head.

One spring the old north wind came south and would not go away. He stayed for many weeks after the flowers should have been coming out and the birds should have been building their nests. It was so cold the leaves would not come out on the bare limbs of the trees. June came, but still the Gulf country looked as it looked during the winter months. The north wind kept blowing the south wind out over the Gulf, and because of this the spring weather would not come.

Finally the young south wind became tired of staying over the Gulf so long. He made up his mind to gather all his power and to enter into a great fight with the north wind that had driven him from his home. Filling his lungs with all the air he could hold, the south wind rushed across the water toward the land. He hit the north wind a mighty blow. When the two winds locked themselves in each other's arms and began howling in each other's faces the Indians ran into

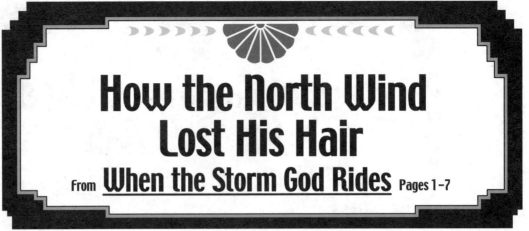

How the North Wind Lost His Hair

From **When the Storm God Rides** Pages 1–7

(continued)

their tents, thinking the Storm God was riding over their heads on his thunder bird that breathed out the lightning. The fighting winds knocked around the clouds in the sky and tore them to pieces as they fought. They pulled up trees; they caused great waves to dash on the beach, they whirled birds around in the air, they tore up the snow that lay on the ground. They ran through the trees, they rolled on the earth and they clawed and shrieked.

At last the young south wind began to get the better of the old north wind. The old fellow was out of breath, and because he was out of breath he lost his power. Then the south wind wrapped his arms in the north wind's long gray hair and began whirling him round and round over his head. He whirled him faster and faster. A strange thing happened. Part of the north wind's gray hair broke loose, and he flew howling through the air.

There stood the young south wind with his strong arms full of hair. He was so happy that he began dancing around and swinging the north wind's hair over the trees. The birds sang and the Indians shouted, for they were glad the south wind had come home again. As the south wind danced and whirled around he let the hair loose, and it fell all over the trees, and where it fell it took root. There it grew and still grows today. It is called Spanish moss. It hangs from the magnolia, oak, gum, and other trees in long gray beards that sometimes dip in the streams.

The north wind does not stay in the south any more. When he sees the moss he remembers that fight with the south wind and he leaves as fast as he can.

A Peaceful Resolution

> " We will bury the tomahawk in the earth."
>
> — Sauk Adage meant as a Pledge of Peace

Grades: 1-5

Purpose: To investigate ways to deal with conflict
To develop assertion skills
To develop an understanding of Nature's methods of protection and assertion

Materials: An area with plants or pictures of plants.
Pictures of animals
Peaceful Resolution Worksheet
Peaceful Resolution Journal Sheet
Pencils

Procedures: • Tell the students the following story: The chaparral cock, or road runner, a bird that lives on lizards and snakes, builds a fence of thorns around a sleeping snake. When the hungry bird finds a snake asleep in the sun, he gathers many thorns and builds a corral around the sleeping snake. Then the roadrunner hides beneath a near-by bush and waits. When the rattlesnake awakes, he tries to crawl through the trap, but the thorns prick him. Then the snake strikes at the thorn pricks until he dies of his own poison. When the snake is dead, the roadrunner runs from his hiding place and eats all he wants of his game.
   Discuss: • How did the Chaparral/ roadrunner deal with the rattlesnake?
      • What do you think about the roadrunner?
      • How would you deal with the rattlesnake?

• Look at the plants and animals in nature or in pictures.
   Discuss: • How does the plant or animal protect itself?
         Examples: Plants: bark, thorns, strong smells, bitter taste, camouflage Animals: claws, teeth, strong jaws, loose skin, coloring, runs fast, intelligent
• Brainstorm ways people protect themselves.
• Individually students will complete the Peaceful Resolution Worksheet by writing or drawing their answers.
• Group discussion of answers follows completion of individual work.
• First Grade can verbalize the Worksheet.

Extension: Journal about an experience you had with a bully and how you dealt with the situation.

Peaceful Resolutions

How would you deal with each of the situations?

An older bully is making fun of a younger student in the school cafeteria line.

_____

_____

A bully is chasing away a student who wants to play in the sand box.

_____

_____

A bully is trying to make a classmate give him his lunch money.

_____

_____

A bully is making fun of a student for having new glasses.

_____

_____

 **Activity #17: BELONGING**

Walk the Good Road

> "Walk the good road…Be dutiful, respectful, gentle and modest…
> Be strong with warm, strong heart of the earth."
>
> — Anonymous Male Sioux

Grades: 1-5

Purpose: To identify significant others in one's life that have a positive influence on one's life

Materials: "The Plant That Grows in Trees" from *When The Storm God Rides*
      by Florence Stratton.
Map of My Heart Worksheet
Letter From My Heart Worksheet

Procedures: • Read "The Plant That Grows in Trees."
    Discuss: • What problem did the mistletoe have?
                • How did the thunderbird have a positive influence on
                  the mistletoe?
                • Have you ever had a problem with which you needed help?
                • Who helped you with the problem?
                • How do family, friends, teachers, and other role models
                  influence our lives by their support and closeness?

                • Brainstorm a list of positive influences that may occur because of those special relationships.
                • Ask students to think of those special people in their lives and complete the Map of My Heart Worksheet.
                • On the lines of the worksheet, the student will write the name of the person, the relationship (friend, family, etc.), and what the positive influence has been on his or her life.

Extension: Students will write a letter using the Letter From My Heart Worksheet to one of their special people and share how the relationship has been a positive influence on their lives

Map of My Heart

Letter From My Heart

Dear _____ ,

This is a letter from my heart. You are a special person in my life. Thank you for

_____

_____

_____

_____

_____

Sincerely,

_____

Date _____

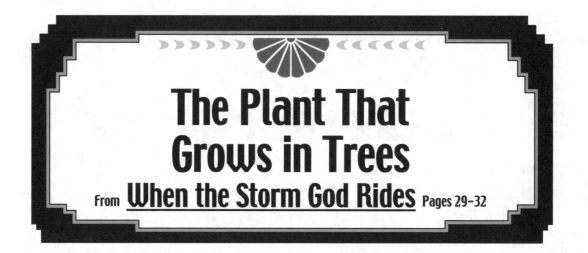

The Plant That Grows in Trees

From <u>When the Storm God Rides</u> Pages 29–32

The mistletoe is a strange little plant. It does not live on the ground with other plants, but always is found growing up in the limbs of tress by itself. Only the birds can reach the little white berries, which appear both in summer and winter. That is why the mistletoe plant is found only in trees. And a bird once put it there because it had pity on the mistletoe.

There was a time when the mistletoe plant did grow on the ground as a small bushy plant. One day when it was growing on the ground a bird called by Indians the thunderbird, which they thought caused the thunder, lit on the mistletoe. The thunderbird was hungry because it could find no berries on other plants. But it found berries on the mistletoe and began to eat them. At last, when the bird had eaten all it wanted of the little waxy white berries, it thanked the bush.

"I am glad you liked my berries," said the mistletoe. "I shall not be here long because I shall soon die." Its leaves were drooping as if it were very tired.

The thunderbird opened its red beak and asked, "Why must you die, little plant?"

"Because I am green the year around" said the mistletoe. "My berries grow in winter when the other berries are gone. Many animals feed on me. They break off my brittle branches when they chew me. I shall not live long." Then the thunderbird took pity on the mistletoe because the bird had liked the little berries. "I shall take you from the ground and put you where the animals that walk on the earth cannot find you any more," said the bird. The thunderbird took the plant in its strong beak and flew up to the top of a mesquite tree. It fastened the roots of the mistletoe into the fork of a limb. Then the bird flew down to the ground and brought back some earth on its beak and packed the earth around the roots of the plant.

"Now, little Mistletoe," said the bird, "you will grow up here in this tree, and the animals will not get your berries."

"Yes, I will grow but when I die my seeds will fall to the ground and they will suffer as I did," said the mistletoe.

The thunderbird laughed and answered: "Oh, but I will see to that." The bird then wiped his long bill, to which stuck some of the berries of the mistletoe, on a limb. "See?" said the bird. "The berries stick on the limb. They will grow there, like you. And whenever other birds eat your berries they will wipe their bills as I do and the seeds of the mistletoe will continue to grow for ever and ever."

And that is why the mistletoe keeps growing in the trees.

56

 **Activity #18: BELONGING**

It's Hard To Say I'm Sorry

> "Lose your temper and you lose a friend;
> lie and you lose yourself."
>
> — Hopi Adage

Grades: 2-5

Purpose: To develop ways of establishing and maintain friendships through conflict resolution

Materials: *The First Strawberry: A Cherokee Story* retold by Joseph Bruchac
It's Hard to Say I'm Sorry Worksheet

Procedures:
- Read aloud the story *The First Strawberry: A Cherokee Story*.
  - **Discuss:**
    - Have you ever had a quarrel with a friend or a loved one?
    - How does it feel for both people? How was it resolved?
    - How do people make up when they have disagreed or hurt one another?
    - What caused the problem for the people in the story?
    - What was each person's viewpoint?
    - Why do you think the Sun helped the man?
    - How did strawberries make a difference to the woman?
    - Of what do strawberries remind the Cherokee people?

- Students will then be asked to think about an argument they have had with someone they cared about.
- Ask them to complete the worksheet It's Hard To Say I'm Sorry.

Extension: Read some conflict scenarios and have the group brainstorm possible solutions to the conflicts.

It is Hard to Say I'm Sorry

Name:_____

On Each Petal Write an Apology.

 **Activity #19: BELONGING**

Kindred Spirit

> "Indians love their friends and kindred,
> and treat them with kindness."
>
> — Cornplanter Seneca, (1736-1836)

Grades: 2-5

Purpose: To develop personal conflict resolutions skills

Materials: *How Chipmunk Got His Stripes* by Joseph Bruchac and James Bruchac
I Can Be A Good Friend Worksheet

Procedures:
- Read the story *How Chipmunk Got His Stripes* to the group.
  Discuss: • What it means to brag and what it means to tease.

- Ask students to role-play several scenarios that involve bragging and teasing.
- Then have the group come up with ways to appropriately react to these scenarios.
- Students will then complete the I Can Be A Good Friend Worksheet.

Extension:
- Students will be placed in groups of two.
- The students will choose two puppets and create a play about dealing with people who tease or brag.

I Can Be A Good Friend

Being a good friend means

_____

_____

_____

Every day I can be a good friend by...

_____

_____

_____

When someone else teases me, I can...

_____

_____

_____

Activity #20: BELONGING

My Feeling Animal

> "In the beginning of all things, wisdom and knowledge were with the animals, for Tirawa, the One Above, did not speak directly to man. He sent certain animals to tell men that he showed himself through the beast, and that from them, and from the stars and the sun and moon should man learn... all things tell of Tirawa."
>
> — Eagle Chief (Letakos-Lesa) Pawnee

Grades: 2-5

Purpose:
- To allow children to explore how they are feeling and to share the feelings with the class
- To provide opportunity for students to feel connected with animals and one another

Materials: *Seya's Song* by Ron Hirschi (ISBN 0-912365-62-5)
Various colors of clay
My Feeling Animal Worksheet

Procedures:
- Read *Seya's Song* aloud.
  - **Discuss:**
    - On her springtime walk what animals did young S'Klallam see?
    - What animals did she see on her fall walk on the beach and her hikes in the mountains?
    - What did Seya, the Grandmother teach S'Klallam?
- Give each child a piece of clay and instruct them to sculpt an animal that represents how they are feeling that day.
- When they are finished, go around the room and have each child show their animal and explain why they sculpted it.

Extension:
- Have each student complete the My Feeling Animal Worksheet to help them explain their feelings more adequately.

- Younger students may draw their answers.

My Feeling Animal

I sculpted a _____ today

because I feel _____.

When I think of (animal) _____, I think

of words such as _____, _____,

and _____.

I feel this way today because _____

_____

_____.

CHAPTER 2
The Need for Mastery

Introduction

Children develop a sense of mastery through opportunities for developing competence. Native American children are taught that someone with more competence is not a rival but a resource and that achievement is sought for personal reasons, not out of competition. The group counselor, through the use of Native American art, literature and dance can build creativity and self-expression. The activity of making Medicine Shields addresses the need for mastery. The Medicine Shield is used as an expression of the unique gifts that the maker wishes to display about his or her current life journey. Every shield carries "medicine," or powerful energy, through art and self-expression. Each shield demonstrates the lessons the maker learned from the four directions on the Medicine Wheel. The Medicine Wheel symbolizes the individual journey each person must take to find his/her own path. The Circle represents the Circle of Life while the center of the circle represents the Eternal Fire. The Eagle, flying toward the East, which is used on the Medicine Shield, is a symbol of strength, endurance and vision. What an excellent symbol of mastery for our children to adopt.

The children may want to include some of the following on their shields: three personally important people, a place which provides security, two enjoyable activities; three words the child would like to have said about him/her, a personality trait of which the child is proud. The use of pet therapy provides the opportunity for the students to build self-esteem and confidence by working with and caring for the animals. Research indicates that there is a positive correlation between the presence of a dog in the lives of students and their success. Keeping pets in the classroom enhances self-esteem (Bergesen, 1989) and early adolescent self-esteem is enhanced by pet ownership (Covert, Whiren, Keith & Nelson, 1985). At the same time that animals motivate learning, the unconditional acceptance by an animal can provide a sense of worth and lovability. Learning to garden through nature therapy can be used to produce vegetables and flowers, which then can be shared. Both the skill of gardening and the internal reward of sharing the products of gardening are sources of pride for the student. Being able to identify and knowing the names of local birds is a cognitive skill, which can be shared with others and bring self-esteem. The development of a child's confidence in his/her ability to interact competently with nature allows our modern day students to acquire the mastery which their Native American peers were more able to achieve naturally.

 **Activity #21: MASTERY**

I Shine Like the Stars!

> "Listen to the stars! We are never alone at night."
>
> — Paul Goble

Grades: 2-6

Purposes: To develop a sense of competence and pride in accomplishment
To teach the use of self-encouragement

Materials: *Star Boy* by Paul Goble (ISBN 0-689-71499-8)
The Star Maiden by Barbara Esbensen & Helen Davie, ISBN 0-316-24955-6
Her Seven Brothers by Paul Goble, ISBN (0-689-71730)
Star Template
Paper for folding into Stars
Colors, markers
Sequins or shiny stickers

Procedures:
- Read one of the books above
- Explain how Indians used the stars to guide and direct them.
- Relate this to older children by having them make a star by folding and writing on it a goal or direction toward which they are heading.
- Call it "Finding Your Own North Star!"
- With younger children, use the Star Template for them to color and decorate with shiny stickers or sequins.
- On all age levels have students write or draw pictures of a positive character quality he/she has.
- Attach strings to the stars and hang them in the room.

Extension: Have students take down their stars from the room to take home to hang in their own rooms. Teach the concept of self-reinforcement and have them use the stars to remind them of their positive qualities and their goals each time they look at their stars.

Star Template

Strong As a Buffalo

"The American Indian is of the soil, whether it be the region of forests, plains, pueblos, or mesas. He fits into the landscape, for the hand that fashioned the continent also fashioned the man for his surroundings. He once grew as naturally as the wild sunflowers; he belongs just as the buffalo belonged…"

— Luther Standing Bear, Oglala Sioux Chief

Grades: 2-5

Purposes: To provide opportunity to learn that there is strength in kindness
To encourage respect for elders, care of weaker creatures, honor in
  dealings with others

Materials: *The Great Buffalo Race* by Barbara Esbensen (ISBN 0316249823)
Light brown and green construction paper
Buffalo Template

Procedures: • Read *The Great Buffalo Race*
  Discuss: • The values of respect for elders, taking care of those who are
     weaker, and being honorable in dealings with others.
    • Point out that there is strength in being kind to others.
    • Was there a time when you were kind to some person or
     animal?
    • How did you feel about that Masterful deed?

  • Students trace the outline of the buffalo on light brown construction paper.
  • Students write or draw on the buffalo about one time they were strong by
   being kind to another person or creature.
  • Students write their names on the back of the buffalo.
  • Students staple the green paper on the bulletin board to make a meadow.
  • Students then stable their buffalo on the green meadow.

Extension: • Invite another class to come to the room to view the buffalo bulletin board.
  • Each student points out their buffalo and tells what they have done to help
   another creature.
  • After about two weeks, students take their buffalos home to display on the
   refrigerator or in their rooms.
  • Send blank buffalos home with instructions to be aware of opportunities to
   be "strong like a buffalo" by doing a good deed.
  • Students are encouraged to make more buffalos at home to remind them
   of their on-going opportunities.

Buffalo Template

Cut out the buffalo shape.
Write or draw on the buffalo about a time when you were strong by being kind.

 **Activity #23: MASTERY**

Buffalo Hide of Pride

> "I looked for the benefits, which would last forever,
> and my face shines with joy…"
>
> — Ten Bears

Grades: 2-5

Purposes: To provide opportunity to develop pride in accomplishments
To provide opportunity to develop pride in abilities
To learn to visualize successful accomplishments
To promote confidence in ability to improve and learn new things

Materials: Pencil
Colors
Brown paper or paper grocery bags
Buffalo Hide Template
The Legend of the Indian Paintbrush by Tomie De Paola (ISBN 0399217770)

Procedures:
- Read *The Legend of the Indian Paintbrush.*
- Discuss the Indian practice of drying buffalo hides and painting on the insides of the hides.
- Make a "buffalo hide" by crushing the brown paper or paper bag several times and then smoothing it out to look like a hide.
- If using a bag, open it along the seam. Cut off the bottom and lay flat. Tear along the edges to make it look rough.
- Or use the Buffalo Hide Template allowing the children to color the hide shape with brown crayons.
- Students draw and color a picture of them doing something they are proud they can accomplish.
- Display the "Hides of Pride" in the room.
- Have students sit in a circle.
- Students close their eyes and visualize themselves doing their accomplishment or skill.
- Emphasize the internal feelings of pride and competency they feel as they visualize.

Extension:
- Students may do another hide to demonstrate something they would like to learn how to do.
- Discussion follows of how to accomplish the goal they have drawn on their hides.

Buffalo Hide Template

Draw a picture of yourself doing something of which you are proud you can do.

 **Activity #24: MASTERY**

Fighting Wolves

> "Which wolf will win?
> The old Cherokee elder replied simply…The one you feed."
>
> — Cherokee Wisdom

Grades: 3-6

Purposes: To acknowledge that all people have negative and positive traits.
To teach the concept that we must nurture the good traits in ourselves and others.

Materials: Wolf Template
Scissors
Markers and colors

Procedures: • Read the following story:

A Cherokee Indian elder was teaching his grandchildren about life. He said to them, "A fight is going on inside me…it is a terrible fight and it is between two wolves. One wolf represents fear, anger, envy, sorrow, regret, greed, arrogance, self-pity, guilt, resentment, inferiority, lies, false pride, superiority, and ego. The other stands for joy, peace, love, hope, sharing, serenity, humility, kindness, benevolence, friendship, empathy, generosity, truth, compassion and faith. This same fight is going on inside of you and inside every other person, too."

The children thought about it for a minute and then one child asked his grandfather, "Which wolf will win?"

The old Cherokee elder replied simply… "The one you feed."

- Discuss the concept of "feeding" as being the same as practicing or repeated behavior, so that the students learn that practicing being brave helps them be brave, etc.
- The students color and cut out two wolf templates.
- One is colored to represent all the negative things about the child.
- The other wolf is colored to represent all the positive things about the child.
- The students then have a play fight between the two wolves at their desk, with strict instructions that the "good" wolf wins.

Extension: • Display good wolves on a bulletin board.
- At the end of each day/session remind the students to read their good wolf before leaving the room.

70

Wolf Templates

Color and then cut out the two wolves.
Color one to be like the parts of you, which you do not like.
Color one to be like the parts of you, which you do like.

 **Activity #25: MASTERY**

Right on Target

> "When Grandmother and Grandfather were young,
> S'Klallam words were with us like the wind,
> the songs of birds, and the swirl of the tide…"
>
> — Ron Hirschi

Grades: 2-5

Purposes: To teach that students can set goals for themselves
To provide opportunity for personal goal-setting
To provide opportunity to experience the pride of being goal-oriented

Materials: *Seya's Song* by Ron Hirschi (ISBN 0-912365-62-5)
Bar of soap for each child
Plastic knives
Arrowhead Patterns
Envelopes

Procedures: • Read *Seya's Song*.
Discuss: • The Salmon's determination to reach their goal of swimming upstream.
• Have you ever had a personal goal you worked for?
• Do you have a goal you would like to reach now?
• Help each student identify one goal.
• Describe arrows and arrowheads. Explain that the tip attached to the end of an arrow shaft is called an arrowhead. The addition of this tip created a weapon and a hunting instrument in order to accomplish the goal of getting food to eat. Arrowheads were made from hard stones. Small pieces were hammered off larger stone then chipped with an antler or bone until the desired shape and sharpness was reached.

• Make soap arrowheads to signify the goal each student has chosen.
• Using the Arrowhead Patterns help students carve arrowheads.
• On the back of their arrowhead have students carve a one-word goal they want to accomplish.
• Provide envelopes into which the students can put their soap arrowheads in order to transport them home.

Extension: • Instruct students to place their soap arrowheads in a special place in their room as a reminder of their goals.
• Weekly, ask for a report of progress made toward their goals.

Soap Arrowhead Templates

Carve an arrowhead shape out of soap.

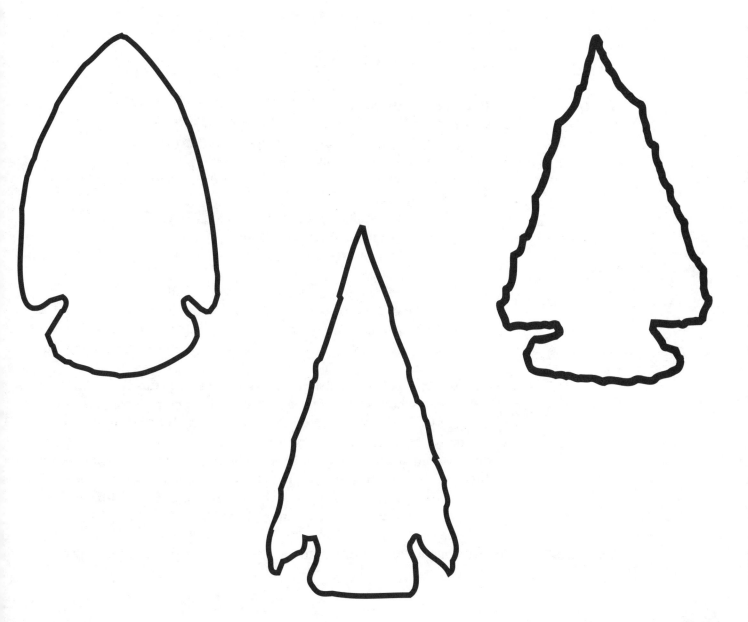

 **Activity #26: MASTERY**

Your Life Road Map

> "As a child I understood how to give,
> I have forgotten this grace since I have become civilized."
> — Luther Standing Bear - Oglala

Grades: 5-8

Purposes: To provide an opportunity to set goals
To provide a sense of mastery by becoming goal-directed

Materials: *The Star Maiden* by Esbensen & Davie (ISBN 0-316-24955-6)
Paper
Pencils
Crayons
Your Life Road Map Worksheet

Procedures: • Read *The Star Maiden.*
Discuss: • What was the goal of the Star Maiden?
• Why did she want to come to the earth?
• What did she like about the Earth?
• How did the young brave help the Star Maiden accomplish her goal?
• What choices did the Star Maiden make?
• How did the Star Maiden finally accomplish her goal?
• Have you ever wanted to do something and talked yourself out of it?
• Who helped you accomplish your goal?
• Does everyone have to always do things the same way?
• Can change be good?
• Do you always get what you want when you believe in yourself?
• How are you like the Star Maiden?
• Have students generate a list of 5 or 6 goals they want to accomplish. It can be within a school year, life goals, family goals, personal goals, etc.
• Have students generate a list of obstacles that might prevent them from accomplishing their goal. For example, students might write procrastination, extra-curricular activities, or major traumas in their life time. These obstacles can be in the form of stop signs, speed bumps, red lights, forks in the road etc.
• Have students generate a list of ways to over come these obstacles.
• Have students make their lists into a "Road Map" of their lives.

Extension: Students might create a time line for when to study or do extra activities.

74

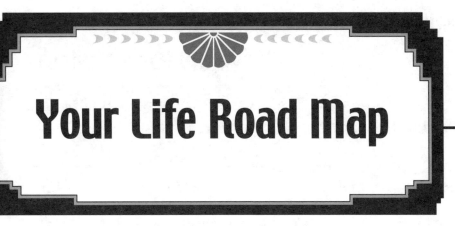

Your Life Road Map

Draw Your Life Road Map.

 **Activity #27: MASTERY**

The Warrior's Vision

"When the Earth is sick, the animals will begin to disappear, when that happens, The Warriors of the Rainbow will come to save them."
— Chief Seattle

Grades: 4-8

Purposes: To provide an opportunity for students to set goals
                 To provide an opportunity for students to feel the mastery of being able to state a personal vision

Materials: *Return to the Land: The Search for Compassion* by Tom Carr
                    ISBN 1-889636-64-9
                 Paper
                 Pencils
                 Markers
                 Staircase to Goals Worksheet

Procedures: • Read #33 Tenacious Animals from *Return to the Land: The Search for Compassion* by Tom Carr
       Discuss: • What does tenacious mean?
                     • Have you ever been tenacious?
                     • What is good about being tenacious?
                     • How does being tenacious help us achieve our goals?
                     • How do we know when to be tenacious or when to give in.
                     • This is a choice we can make.
                     • What kind of choices do you make every day?
                 • Brainstorm some tough choices students might have to face in order to reach their goals.
                 • Have students draw a staircase with 5-6 stairs.
                 • At the top of the stairs, have the students write "Reached my Goal."
                 • On each step have the students write down a choice they will have to make in order to reach their goal.

Extension: • For younger students, write a class goal at the top of the worksheet.
                 • Discuss ways the class can work to achieve the goal.
                 • List the goals
                 • Draw pictures of the class working on the goals

Staircase to Goals

This is a Picture of My Class
Working Together on Our Goal

Activity #28: MASTERY

The Rough Faced Girl

> "I was warmed by the sun, rocked by the winds and sheltered by the trees as other Indian babes. I was living peaceably when people began to speak bad of me. Now I can eat well, sleep well and be glad. I can go everywhere with a good feeling."
>
> — Geronimo

Grades: K-5

Purposes: To encourage positive self-image
To encourage inner strength
To encourage faith

Materials: *Rough Faced Girl* by Martin & Shannon (ISBN 0590469320)
Paper
Markers
The Rough Faced Girl Worksheet

Summary: In this Algonquin Indian version of the Cinderella story, two domineering sisters set out to marry the "rich, powerful, and supposedly handsome" Invisible Being. But first they must prove that they can see him. They cannot, but their mistreated younger sister the Rough-Face Girl—so called because the sparks from the fire have scarred her skin—can, for she sees his "sweet yet awesome face" all around her. He then appears to her, reveals her true hidden beauty and marries her.

Procedures:
- Read *The Rough Faced Girl.*

Discuss:
  - The self-concept of the Rough-Face Girl, her haughty sisters, and the warrior.
  - How a person reacts to another often influences how a person feels about himself/herself.
  - Focus upon the traits of faith, courage, and inner beauty.
- Have students fill out the Me and The Rough-Faced Girl Worksheet comparing themselves to The Rough Faced Girl.

Extension:
- Younger students may draw, rather than write on the Rough-Faced Girl Worksheet.

- Have students write their own "Cinderella" stories.

Me and The Rough Faced Girl

Characteristics of the Rough-Faced Girl:

Characteristics I have that are like the Rough-Faced Girl:

Characteristics of the Rough-Faced Girl that I would like to develop:

Activity #29: MASTERY

A Green Thumb

> "The sun and the moon look at us, and the ground gives us food."
> — Chief Blackfoot

Grades: 2-5

Purposes: To develop self-esteem
To develop a sense of connection with nature
To develop an ability to grow and take care of a plant

Materials: *Return to the Land: The Search for Compassion* by Tom Carr
ISBN 1-889636-64-9
Styrofoam cups
Colored Markers
Potting Soil
Flower Seeds
Water
Plant Growth Chart

Procedures: • Read #69 Queen of the Night from *Return to the Land: The Search for Compassion* by Tom Carr
Discuss: • Why was Amber looking for a special flower?
• What did Amber do with the flower when she found it?
• Have you ever given a flower to someone special to you?
• Have you ever grown a plant?
• What does it take for a plant to grow?
• Discuss the roles we will play in getting the plant to grow.
• Go over the growth chart reminding the students of what they will need to do every day to help their plant grow.
• Students write their names on their cups and decorate the cups with colored markers.
• Plant the seeds and keep the planted seeds in the room near a window.
• Chart the growth progress weekly.

Extension: • Plant the seeds and have the students take the plants home.
• Have the students bring their charts in weekly and discuss how well their plants are growing.

Plant Growth Chart

What to do:	Monday	Tuesday	Wednesday	Thursday	Friday	Saturday	Sunday
Water the plant							
Make sure the plant is getting enough sunlight							
Measure the plant for growth							
Comments on how the plant is doing							

Activity #30: MASTERY

Determined Responses

> "The earth and myself are of one mind."
>
> — Chief Joseph

Grades: 4-5

Purposes: To recognize that students have a choice of how to respond to problems
To provide students with the opportunity to think through problems
and decide how they will react

Materials: *Big Moon Tortilla* by Joy Crowley ISBN#1-59078-037
Determined Response Work Sheet
Pen or Pencil

Procedures:
- Read *Big Moon Tortilla.*

Discuss:
- What does it mean to be a tree, rock, mountain lion, and an eagle.
- In the book we are given options of how we respond to the problem in different ways like a tree, rock, mountain, or an eagle.
- Think of a time in your life when you responded to problems like these.

- Using the Determined Response Work Sheet, students may either write or draw their responses.
- Once group members have completed the activity allow them to discuss their experiences.
- Have the group members discuss how they can apply this principle of problem solving to their daily lives.

Extension:
- Over the next week have students journal problems that occur.
- They are to journal whether they responded like a tree, rock, mountain lion or eagle.
- Next session discuss whether or not these responses were helpful.

Determined Responses

The time that I was like a tree was when….	The time that I was like a rock was when…
The time that I was like a mountain lion was when….	The time that I was like an eagle was when…

Hidden Treasures

> "Every part of this Earth is sacred to my people, every shining pine needle, every sandy shore, every mist in the dark woods, every meadow, every humming insect…"
>
> — Chief Seattle (Seathl) Duwamish-Suquamish, 1788-1866

Grades: 3-5

Purposes: To develop a sense of mastery
To improve observation skills
To increase interest in the natural environment
To develop teamwork skills

Materials: *Return to the Land: The Search for Compassion* by Tom Carr
    ISBN 1-889636-64-9
Walk In Peace Worksheet
Poster Board
Glue
Scissors
My Own Hidden Treasures Worksheet

Procedures: • Read #29 The Sign of the Fox: Good or Bad? In *Return to the Land: The Search for Compassion* by Tom Carr

Discuss: • Tell students that there are many hidden treasures in the outdoors and each one has a special place in nature.
  • However, these items are often overlooked and never noticed. Each treasure is diverse and unique.
• The students will then form pairs and begin the scavenger hunt.
• When the hunt is over, the group will discuss the treasures that they found and what makes them special.

Extension: • Students will journal or draw about an overlooked, special trait that they possess using the My Own Hidden Treasures Worksheet.
• Create a collage with some of the items from the scavenger hunt.

Hidden Treasures

❑ Wild Flowers
❑ Dead tree
❑ Pine cone
❑ Berries
❑ Vine
❑ Poison ivy
❑ Stream or creek
❑ Blade of grass
❑ Clover leaf
❑ Moss
❑ Pine tree
❑ Seeds or seed pod
❑ Eroded soil
❑ Smooth/shiny rock
❑ Mud
❑ Grain of sand
❑ Fern
❑ Y-shaped twig
❑ Trash
❑ Pine needles
❑ Acorn or other nuts
❑ Tree with blossoms
❑ Hole in a tree
❑ Pond area in a creek
❑ Dark or light green leaf
❑ Small pebble
❑ Unusual shaped leaf
❑ Rocks with many colors
❑ Different shades of green
   or brown
❑ Dew on a flower or leaf
❑ Fungus on a tree
❑ Shows next season is
   coming

❑ Animal tracks
❑ Worm
❑ Caterpillar
❑ Squirrel
❑ Bird
❑ Ant
❑ Butterfly or moth
❑ Snail
❑ Beetle
❑ Feather
❑ Lizard
❑ Ladybug
❑ Spider web
❑ Birds nest
❑ Insects on a tree
❑ Deer tracks
❑ Animal hole in the ground
❑ Deer
❑ Frog
❑ Leaf with insect holes
❑ Evidence of the presence
   of animals
❑ Evidence of the presence
   of people

LISTEN TO:
❑ Leaves under your feet
❑ Wind in the trees
❑ Sound of a bee
❑ Birds singing
❑ Cricket
❑ Water running in a creek
❑ Noises in the woods

FEEL:
❑ Tree bark
❑ Prickly plant
❑ Wet mud
❑ Rotten wood
❑ Wind blowing on face
❑ Texture of various rocks

SMELL:
❑ Pine tree
❑ Flower
❑ Mud
❑ Green grass
❑ Fresh air
❑ Cedar tree

WATCH:
❑ Animals eating
❑ Leaf falling to the ground
❑ Spider web w/insect
❑ Ant moving something
❑ Wind blowing the leaves
❑ Fish jumping
❑ Clouds going by
❑ For something funny
❑ For something unusual
❑ Sunlight coming through
   trees
❑ Sunrise or sunset
❑ Stars in the sky
❑ Lightning Bugs
❑ Reflection in the water
❑ Trail markers
❑ Animal homes
   or shelters

My Own Hidden Treasures

Journal or draw about some special trait
or quality you possess which is sometimes overlooked.

Activity #32: MASTERY
Silence is Golden

> "Listen to all the teachers of the woods. Watch the trees, the animals, and all living things—you will learn more from them than books."
>
> — Joe Coyhis Stockbridge-Munsee

Grades: 2-5

Purpose: To gain an awareness of self
To improve listening skills
To foster an appreciation for Nature

Materials: *Return to the Land: The Search for Compassion* by Tom Carr
ISBN 1-889636-64-9
Clipboard
Pencils
Silence is Golden Worksheet

Procedures:
• Read #37 Sacred Deer Hunting from *Return to the Land: The Search for Compassion* by Tom Carr
   Discuss: • Why was silence vital to the Native American's?
   • What kind of punishment was given to a warrior who was careless and made noise on a hunt?
• Take students outside and have everyone sit in a circle.
• Explain: Nature is a special place where people from many Native American cultures go to be close to Earth and to better know themselves.
• Being quiet is very important for hearing well.
• Let's see how well you can listen.

• The students will sit and listen to the sounds of nature for about 10 minutes (depending on attention span).
• Have each student find their own spot outside to complete their worksheet in silence.

Extension: • Students will draw what they pictured in their minds as they were listening to nature.

Silence is Golden

 What did you hear first?

 What sounds did you hear after listening for a while?

 What sounds did you like?

 Which sounds did people make?

 Which sounds did animals make?

© YouthLight, Inc.

Activity #33: MASTERY
The Animal Within

> "Oh, Eagle, come with wings outspread in the sunny skies.
> Oh, Eagle, come and bring us peace, they gentle peace.
> Oh, Eagle, come and give new life to us who pray.
> Remember the circle of the sky, the stars, and the brown eagle,
> the great life of the Sun, the you within the nest.
> Remember the sacredness of things."
>
> — Pawnee Prayer

Grades: 2-5

Purpose: To acknowledge personal qualities
To acknowledge special qualities that one would like to posses

Materials: "The Teachings of the Eagle" from *Keepers of the Animals: Native American Stories and Wildlife Activities for Children* by Michael J. Caduto and Joseph Bruchac (ISBN # 1-55591-386-5)
If I Were An Animal Worksheet
If I Were An Animal Drawing Sheet
Clay

Procedures: • Read the story "The Teachings of the Eagle."
   Discuss: • This is a Pawnee story.
        • Have you ever seen an eagle? Where?
        • Why do so many people use the bald eagle as a symbol?
        • What qualities make the eagle special?
• Have student close their eyes and take a few deep breaths. Ask them to imagine that they are animals.
• The students will then complete the If I Were An Animal Worksheet
   Discuss: • What animal did you choose to be?
        • What makes that animal special?

Extension: • Students draw their animal on the If I Were An Animal Drawing Sheet.
• Students create a clay sculpture of their animal.

If I Were An Animal...

Choose an animal you would like to be.
Pretend you are this animal for the remaining questions.

My Name_____ **Animal's Name**_____

1. Describe your natural enemies. How do you protect yourself from your enemies? _____

_____

2. What do you eat? _____

_____

3. Where do you live? _____

_____

4. What special qualities do you have (feathers, scales, fur, etc.)?

_____

_____

_____

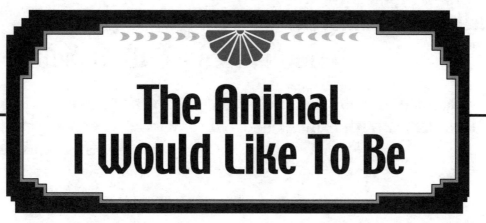

The Animal I Would Like To Be

This is a picture of the animal I would like to be, if I were an animal.

 **Activity #34: MASTERY**

The Names I Call Myself

"Indian names were either characteristic nicknames given in a playful spirit, deed names, birth names, or such as have a religious or symbolic meaning."
— Ohiyesa (Charles Eastman), Santee Sioux, 1858-1939

Grades: 3-5

Purposes: To gain an understanding of individual strengths
To gain an appreciation for self

Materials: *A Boy Called Slow: The True Story of Sitting Bull* by Joseph Bruchac
(ISBN 0-698-11616-X)
Naming Worksheet
When I Grow Up Letter

Procedures: • Read *A Boy Called Slow: The True Story of Sitting Bull.*
• The group will then discuss the story and their reactions to it.
• Students complete the Naming Worksheet and share with the group.

Discuss: • Do you think Sitting Bull knew what he wanted to be when he grew up?
• What plans might Sitting Bull have made to make sure that he dream came true?
• Did Sitting Bull have to have any special training or education to do what he did?
• What do you think it was like?
• What kind of advice do you think Sitting Bull might give you?

Extension: • Using the When I Grow Up form, have students write a letter to themselves in which they tell what they hope to do when they grow up.
• They must also tell how they hope to meet those goals.
• Suggest that they illustrate the final copy of their letters.

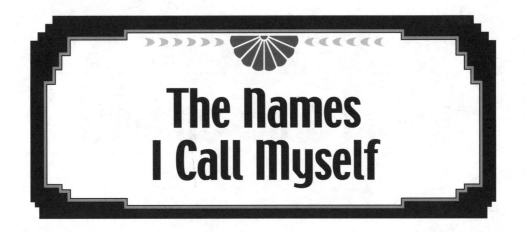

The Names I Call Myself

I call myself _____

I also call myself _____

I wonder if I will _____

I would like to hear _____

I would like to see _____

I want some day to be _____

Then I will call myself _____

Some times I feel _____

Some times I worry about _____

Sometimes I am very sad about _____

I call myself _____

(The first line of the poem repeated)

When I Grow Up Letter

Dear _____ ,
(own name)

When I grow up, I hope to

_____

_____

I plan to accomplish this by

_____

_____

This is a picture of me doing this.

Activity #35: MASTERY

"Help Me, Please" Is a Sign of Strength

> "If a man loses anything and goes back and looks carefully for it he will find it."
>
> — Sitting Bull

Grades: K-3

Purpose: To learn to ask for help

Materials: *Little Sky Eagle and the Pumpkin Drum* by Mildred Feague
(ISBN73-123805)
Pumpkin Template
It's OK to Ask For Help Worksheet
Pumpkin Thank You Notes

Procedures: • Read *Little Sky Eagle and the Pumpkin Drum.*
   Discuss: • What kinds of things could Little Sky Eagle do for himself?
      • In what ways was he independent?
      • What was his dream about the pumpkin?
      • Where did he carry the pumpkin?
      • How did he carry the pumpkin after he met the Singing Toads?
      • How did the Snake Dancer and the Antelope Men help him with the Rattling Rattler in his dreams?
      • How did his mother help him at the end of the story?
   • Using the Pumpkin Template the students draw a picture of something that is hard for them to do for which they need help.
   • Complete the It's OK to Ask For Help Worksheet.

Extension: • Write Thank You Pumpkins/Notes to the helpers of the students.
   • Send the Pumpkin pictures home with the students, with Thank You Notes/Pumpkins to the person who helps them with the activity drawn on the Pumpkin Templates.

It's OKAY to Ask for Help!

Name _____ Date _____

Sometimes it's tough to ask for help. Sometimes, people think that asking for help shows weakness. But does it? Think of times that you have had to ask for help. Explain how asking for help was a good thing.

_____

_____

_____

_____

Draw a picture of a time when someone helped you, or you helped someone else.

[ ]

How did you feel when you helped someone else, or someone else helped you?

_____

96

This is a Really Big Pumpkin
With Which I Need Help

Draw a picture of you doing
something with which
you need help.

Thanks for your help.

This is a pumpkin/note to say thank you
for helping me with

_____

_____

Signed _____

Activity #36: MASTERY
The Wolf Keeps Me Safe

> "The death of fear is in doing what you fear to do."
>
> — Sequchie Comingdeer

Grades: K-5

Purpose: To demonstrate that students can overcome fear
To illustrate how positive thoughts can help to cope with fear

Materials: *Dream Wolf* by Paul Goble (ISBN 0-02-736585-9)
Crayons, markers, map pencils
Wolf Worksheet

Procedures:
- Read *Dream Wolf* by Paul Goble.
  - **Discuss:**
    - What was scary for Tiblo and Tanksi when they climbed into the hills alone?
    - How did they feel when it got dark?
    - When Tanksi began to cry, what did Tiblo do to help them with their fears. (Spoke of happy things.)
    - How was the wolf in Tiblo's dream a friend to the children?
    - How did the wolf help the children in the morning?
    - Of what are you afraid?
    - Is it okay to be afraid of things?
    - Does it make you a wimp or sissy?
- Distribute Wolf Worksheet and art materials.
- Have students draw themselves overcoming these fears.
  - **Discuss:**
    - How might you feel if you overcame their fears?
    - Who is the Wolf in your life (the person or things, which can keep you safe)?
    - The Wolf could be happy and safe thoughts inside your head, just as Tiblo used happy thoughts when he and Tanksi were afraid in the hills at night.

Extension:
- Make a Wolf Bulletin Board with the Wolf drawings.

The Wolf
Keeps Me Safe

This is a picture of what
makes me afraid.

This is a picture of what
keeps me safe.

Activity #37: MASTERY

Old Quanah's Gift

> "We will be known forever by the tracks we leave."
>
> — Dakota

Grades: 4-6

Purpose: To demonstrate the values of hard work
To provide opportunity to take pride in a job well done

Materials: "Old Quanah's Gift" in *When The Storm God Rides* by Florence Stratton.
Yarn of many colors
Small looms
Or
Strips of construction paper of many colors

Procedures:
- Read "Old Quanah's Gift."
  - **Discuss:**
    - Old Quanah's work ethic: responsibility, diligence, pride in his work.
    - Is there some work or activity in which you take pride?
    - At what do you like to work hard?
    - What did the villagers think of Old Quanah's weaving ability?
    - What did the villagers keep asking Old Quanah?
    - Old Quanah left them more than a blanket and new flowers, he left them his example of hard work and craftsmanship.
- Students weave their own blankets either using the small looms and yarn or the colored strips of construction paper.
- Students are instructed to think about the things they like to do well as they weave their "blankets" and what qualities of Old Quanah they would like to develop within themselves.

Extension:
- Display the "blankets" in the room or in a display case in the hall.
- Students brainstorm words to describe Mastery to be written in large letters to be displayed in the case with the blankets.

Old Quanah's Gift

From **When the Storm God Rides** Pages 114-122

Why did old Quanah, the blanket weaver known among all the Indians of the southwest country, give so much time and care to a blanket, which he had not finished after many years of work? The Indians of his tribe asked this question, but old Quanah always smiled and shook his head. Some day, he said, he would tell them.

Quanah, who had spent many years in the making of blankets, knew better than any other Indian how to put into them the beauty of color and form. He had once been a brave warrior, a fighter who took pride in his use of bow and arrow, and in following the trails of animals and enemies of the tribe. But when at last a poisoned arrow struck him in the leg and caused him to be crippled, he had to stay in camp and could no longer fight. Quanah, the proud fighter, did not like this. He did not like staying at home with the women of the tribe.

Because Quanah refused to be idle he at last began to make blankets, and because he was a man who took pride in his work he learned the art of making blankets with great care. Through forest and swamp he went seeking strange herbs, roots and flowers with which to make dyes that other blanket weavers had never used. He found out what were the best fleeces and fibers to use in making blankets smooth and warm and strong. He always made his own dyes with great care. He wove his blankets each time with different patterns, so that no two were alike. And he worked so carefully that he became known everywhere for his blankets.

Indian chiefs of other tribes heard of him and came to see him at work or to buy blankets from him. Other blanket makers came from many miles away to watch him make his dyes and weave the colored fleeces into his lovely designs. Quanah gladly tried to show them what he knew, but when they had gone away and tried to do as he had told them they found that they could not. They did not have Quanah's art, his magic touch.

For years Quanah worked. His blankets became famous. Some looked like the rosy clouds and mists of dawn. Others had the vivid colors of the red and yellow prairie flowers. Each one he made seemed to be better than the one before.

But there was one blanket, which Quanah worked on year after year without finishing. Each day he would work a little bit on it, but slowly it grew until the Indians could see that in its center there would be a great golden, shining sun. Quanah was very careful in making the dyes for this blanket and weaving colors slowly into place. Around the bright sun other colors of sunset were woven. The red and purple of evening clouds were there, and also the yellow hues of thin clouds that were close to the golden sun. The Indians kept asking him what he was going to do with this wonderful blanket, but Quanah always smiled and said he would tell them when it was finished. Years went by. Quanah kept working, until he was so old that his fingers shook when he worked.

At last one day the Indians found the old blanket maker lying on a mat with his wrinkled face turned up to the skies. He was dying. But beside him lay the wonderful blanket, finished. Its many shades seemed to change as the Indians took it carefully in their fingers. The sun in its middle burned with the brightness of the real sun in the sky, and all the gleaming colors around it seemed to flow like the waters of the river when the changing lights of sunset struck them. As the Indians held this lovely blanket they looked down at old Quanah and saw that he was dying. Then they began to wail or to beat their breasts, because they knew they would never have another blanket maker like him.

But Quanah slowly opened his eyes and whispered to them: "My blanket is finished at last. Now I will tell you why I have made it with so much care and have put so much beauty into it. It is for the most worthy of our tribe. The man who has done most for his people is to have this blanket, so that our children may know that it is a fine thing for them to become good members of our tribe." And with this old Quanah's voice failed and he died.

Soon the Indians began to ask one another who should have the blanket. Who had done the most for his tribe? The chief called a council to decide the question. One man who was a brave warrior was pointed out as the right man. Another who was a great hunter of game was named. But the Indians could not agree about it. Some wanted this man; others wanted that one.

At length the chief held up his hand for silence. "We have forgotten the man who has really done most for us," said the chief pointing towards the still body of old Quanah lying before the tribal alter. "There he lies. Quanah himself should have the blanket. Is he not famous everywhere? Did he not make our tribe known far and wide?"

"Yes, Quanah must have the blanket!" cried the Indians. No longer did they argue. The old man who had made it was the very one who should have it, for he had done most for them. They did not like to see the lovely blanket laid away in the earth from all eyes, but they tenderly wrapped Quanah's body in its folds and then laid the old man and his finest work in the ground. Then each member of the tribe placed upon the new grave a large stone. At last they went away. They were sad because Quanah had died and because they could see the blanket no more.

But they were to see something as wonderful as a blanket. The spirit of Quanah, wishing them to have something of the beauty, which they had buried with the blanket, gave its colors back to them in the form of a new kind of flower that began to grow among the stones on the grave. In these flowers were the same reds and yellows and browns, which were woven into the blanket. There were the same hues of sunset in the flower petals. They were the same colors, which white men later found in these flowers. White men now call them wild gaillardia, or blanket flowers, or fire wheels. Thus it happened that old Quanah gave a new flower to the world.

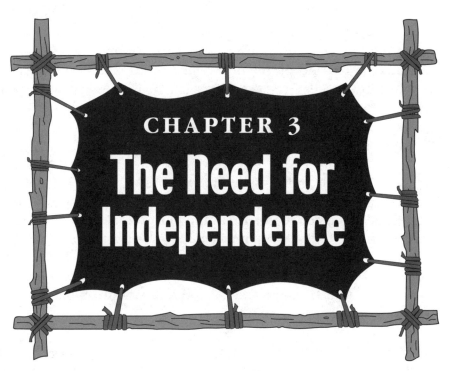

CHAPTER 3
The Need for Independence

Introduction

The Native American practice of encouraging children to make decisions, solve problems, and be responsible, by adults who model and teach responsible behavior, produces children who feel respected and powerful. Children who feel strong and independent have no need to disobey in order to demonstrate independence or to bully others for respect or to attain power. Group counselors can provide for this need for independence by teaching self-management, as well as the recognition and the management of emotions, behaviors and thoughts. Group exercises in which the children can help decide on rules and group procedures impart a sense of self-management. Other activities, such as the Native American practice of renaming the child with an animal name or name from nature, which denotes values of strength and courage, demonstrate respect for each child.

The Harmony Circle is another activity suggested by Garrett and Crutchfield (1997), which can be used to teach the blending of independence and belonging. In the Harmony Circle, each child selects an instrument to play from among wood blocks, bells, sticks, plastic bottles and rattles. The children then follow the leader who establishes a rhythm allowing a song to be improvised. The concepts of cooperation and harmony can be discussed along with how important each person is to the creation of the whole song.

The Medicine Bag activity is another vehicle for teaching the concept of each child having a "special gift from Mother Earth." The child makes and decorates a cloth bag into which a symbol of his/her own special talents is placed. The child is told that these special gifts are their "personal way of life," referred to as "medicine" by Native Americans. If allowed in your school, pet therapy provides the child with the opportunity to care for the animals in the group setting, giving the child a sense of control and responsibility, as does allowing the children to take turns walking the leashed animal. Learning to appropriately set limits for the pet leads easily into lessons on how to set limits with peers. Children who have learned to manage pets can be more assertive with peers, developing feelings of self-respect and independence. The next natural progression is for the counselor to draw a parallel between the child's learning to control his/her own behavior, just as the dog learns to execute a "long down stay." Encouraging the child to decide on an object of nature he/she will bring into the group to talk about at the next session or decide where the counselor and children will walk outside as they talk, provides the children a sense of self-management and autonomy.

Activity #38: INDEPENDENCE
Five Cohonks Ago

> "I have made myself what I am."
>
> — Tecumseh (1810)

Grades: 3-6

Purpose: To promote independence by developing organizational skills.
To develop organizational skills to aid in tracking and completing
school assignments.

Materials: *Return to the Land: The Search for Compassion* by Tom Carr
ISBN 1-889636-64-9
My Personal Plan for Peace Through Organization Assignment Sheets
Pen or Pencil

Procedures:
- Read #27 Napoleon's Downfall? He Didn't Check the Weather Report
from *Return to the Land: The Search for Compassion* by Tom Carr
  Discuss:
  - How did the Native Americans use the animals to help them
  predict the weather?
  - Even the Native Americans of long ago needed organization.
  - What is the meaning of organization?
  - How can being organized be helpful in our lives?
  - Contrast the anxious feeling that being disorganized creates
  as compared to the peaceful feeling of being organized.
  - What are the different areas in your lives in which you are dis
  organized?
  - Which areas would you like to be more organized?
- Counselor discusses organizational tools such as a planner, assignment
sheet, and daily calendar.
- Practice filling out an assignment sheet and discuss appropriate time in
class to fill this out.
- Counselor will teach how to use the assignment sheet in prioritizing when
to do assignments.

Extension:
- Have the students keep the assignment sheets for one week.
- In the next session discuss whether or not the assignment sheets have
been helpful and, if so, how.
- Discuss the feelings of anxiety vs. peacefulness in relation to
disorganization and organization.

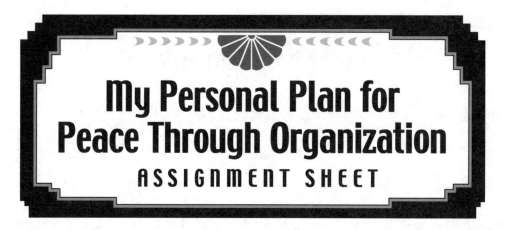

My Personal Plan for Peace Through Organization
ASSIGNMENT SHEET

Subject	Monday	Tuesday	Wednesday	Thursday	Friday
Math					
Science					
Language Arts					
Social Studies					
Other					

Activity #39: INDEPENDENCE
Your Inner Animal

> "What I am, I am"
>
> — Sitting Bull

Grades: 2-6

Purpose: To provide opportunity to evaluate what qualities make them strong and unique

To provide an opportunity to improve self-esteem

Materials: *Return to the Land: The Search for Compassion* by Tom Carr
ISBN 1-889636-64-9
Pictures of Animals
Animal Worksheet
Pen or pencil

Procedures:
- Read #114 Dakota Three Toes from *Return to the Land: The Search for Compassion* by Tom Carr
  - **Discuss:**
    - How did Dakota Three Toes get his name?
    - Describe how Native Americans took names from Nature.
    - Brainstorm some names taken from animals such as Big Bear, Running Deer, Brave Eagle, etc.
- Write these names on the Board.
- Show pictures of animals from all over the world and discuss how thy all possess unique qualities that help them survive and contribute to Nature.
- Brainstorm positive qualities about various animals, writing the animal's name on the board with the quality beside the name.
- Group members will choose an animal they feel can represent them.
- Using the animal worksheet have the group members describe themselves, the animal they chose, and in the center the qualities that they both share.
- Once group members have completed the activity allow those who choose to share with the group.
- Younger students can draw themselves and the animal on the Animal Worksheet

Extension:
- Students will discuss the qualities of strength they possess and how it is important that each member has different qualities.
- Students journal about qualities that they would like to strengthen including discussion of members in their family or friends who exhibit those qualities.

Your Inner Animal Worksheet

Description of You	Description of Animal Chosen

In this box, draw/list qualities both you and the animal possess.

Activity #40: INDEPENDENCE
Reading the Signs

> "May we be strong in spirit and equal to our Fathers of another day
> in reading the signs accurately and interpreting them wisely."
> — Unknown speaker addressing the National Congress of Americans

Grades: 3-6

Purpose: To provide opportunity to read the signs of stress accurately and to interpret
them wisely as the need to relax
To gain an understanding of stress and how our bodies show stress
To learn progressive muscle relaxation as a skill to help cope with stress
To provide the realization that Nature can be relaxing

Materials: *Return to the Land: The Search for Compassion* by Tom Carr
ISBN 1-889636-64-9
Relaxing music/Nature sounds tape
Progressive Muscle Relaxation Training Script
My Stressed Body Work Sheet
My Relaxed Body Work Sheet
Crayons

Procedures:
- Read #29 The Sign of the Fox: Good or Bad? In *Return to the Land: The Search for Compassion* by Tom Carr
  - **Discuss:**
    - Just as Native Americans were taught to read signs of Nature, we can read the signs of our stressed bodies.
    - What is stress?
    - What about Nature is relaxing to you?
    - Has anyone has ever felt "stressed out?"
    - Our bodies tell us that we are stressed with signs like a fast heartbeat, sweating, tightness in the stomach, being unable to fall asleep at night, etc.
- Students share times they may have felt these symptoms.
- Students use the My Relaxed Body and My Stressed Body Worksheets to illustrate their relaxed and stressed states.
- Students are guided through the relaxation training exercise.
- Students sit in chairs with plenty of space between them with eyes closed while counselor reads the script or students can lie on the floor.
- Student reactions are shared after the activity.

Extension:
- Students are given a tape made by the Counselor to practice at home for a week and report the results after a week of use.

Progressive Muscle Relaxation Training Script

 Wrinkle your forehead and your nose, and close your eyes very tightly. Now relax your face and feel the muscles soften. Enjoy the feeling of a relaxed face.

 Put both your arms out straight. Make fists. Tighten your whole arms from your hand to your shoulder. Squeeze tighter and tighter, still. Squeeze even tighter! Now, gradually relax your arms, bending them at the elbows; relax so that your arm is resting on your lap in a comfortable position. Just let all the tension flow out of your arms through your fingertips. Feel the tension flowing out through your fingertips and away from your body.

 Now, lift your legs, turn your toes in towards you, and tighten your whole legs. Squeeze tighter, tighter. Squeeze even tighter! Gradually relax and lower your legs until your feet are squarely on the floor, bending your knee as you relax. Enjoy the heavy, relaxed feeling as all the tension flows out of your body through your legs, and into the floor through your feet.

 Tighten your stomach, pulling it in, making it hard. Harder, harder. Even harder! Gradually relax your stomach muscles. Relaxed, loose muscles feel so good. Just enjoy that calm relaxed feeling in your stomach muscles.

 Now just rest comfortably in a completely relaxed state. Notice if there is any left over tension in your body. If so, just breathe into that space and breathe that tension away. Just drifting in a completely relaxed condition.

 Now begin to wiggle fingers and toes just a little bit. Moving just a bit to begin to move back into your normal state of being. Do not forget to thank yourself for allowing yourself to manage your stress by deeply relaxing.

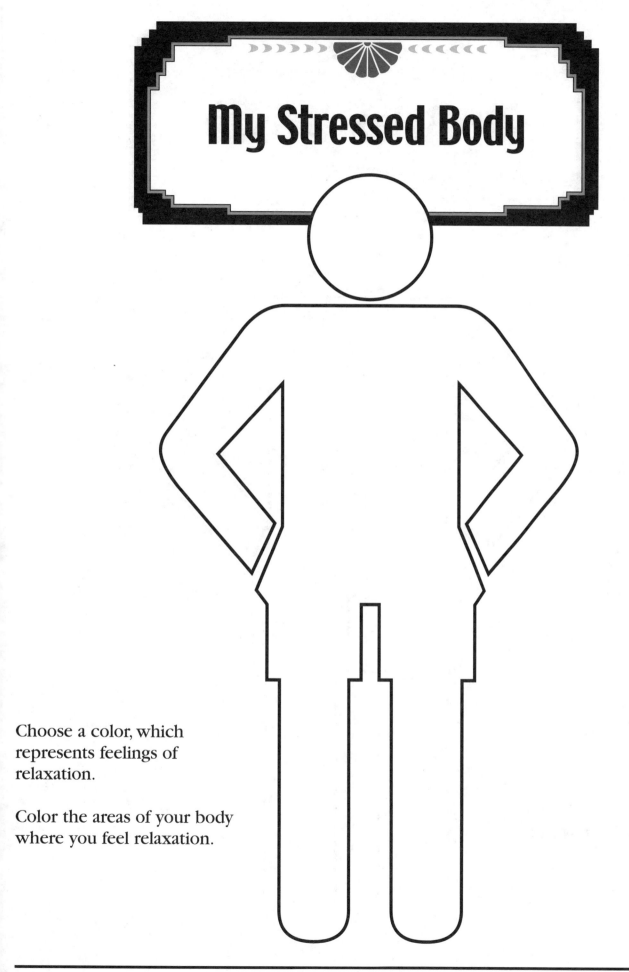

My Stressed Body

Choose a color, which represents feelings of relaxation.

Color the areas of your body where you feel relaxation.

My Relaxed Body

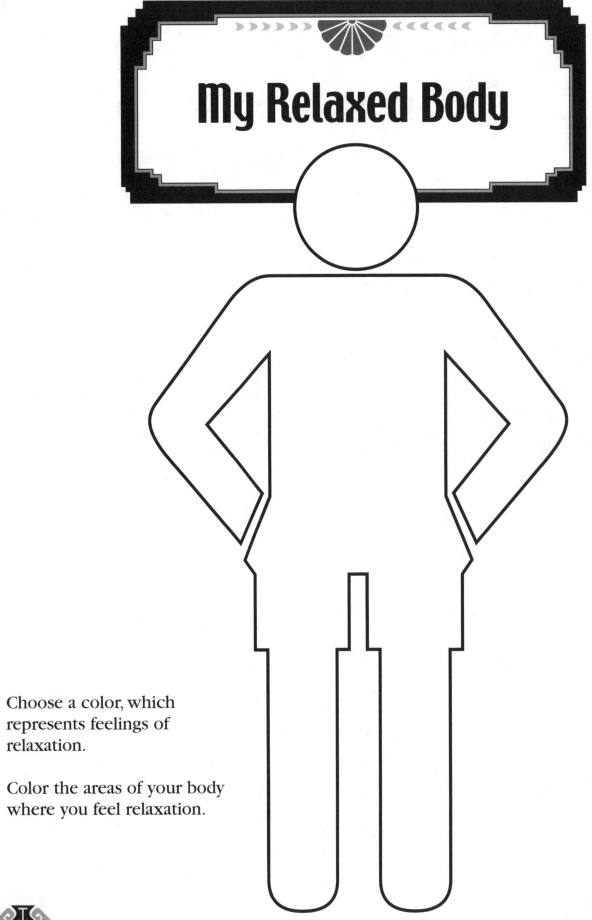

Choose a color, which represents feelings of relaxation.

Color the areas of your body where you feel relaxation.

Activity #41: INDEPENDENCE

Pinduli

> "All things share the same breath - the beast, the tree,
> the man, the air shares its spirit with all the life it supports."
>
> — Mourning Dove Salish, 1888-1936

Grades: K-3

Purpose: To promote self-acceptance
                 To promote personal growth
                 To promote a positive body-image

Materials: *Pinduli* by Janell Cannon (ISBN 0152046682)
                 Pencil & crayons
                 Pinduli Work Sheet

Summary: One hot afternoon, Mama Hyena and her child go hunting. Pinduli promises to stay close by, but then trots off. She comes upon a pack of wild dogs, a lion, and a zebra, which all tease her about her looks. She rolls in the dirt until her striped coat is a pale gray and her ears are pinned back. The animals think that she is a "ghost" that has come for them. All of the creatures then confess that they teased the young hyena because another animal had made fun of them. The "ghost" understands and advises them to "find your tormentors and make peace....And always leave a bit of every meal as an offering." By story's end, the animals have reconciled. With all the food offerings left, Pinduli and her mother never have to scrounge around looking for meals.

Procedures: • Read *Pinduli*
     Discuss: • The lessons of self-acceptance and self-reliance of Pinduli.
                  • How she used the resources around her in nature to help her.
                  • How she did not use violence to teach the other animals a lesson.
                  • How Pinduli solved her problem by herself.
                 • Ask students to write about a time when they solved a problem by themselves. Younger students draw.
                 • Have the students share their stories and the feeling that come along with being independent.
                 • For Kindergarten, verbalize worksheet.

Extension: • Have the students write stories of problems they have solved independently and make them into a class book for others to read.

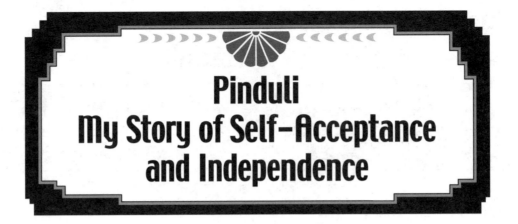

Pinduli
My Story of Self-Acceptance and Independence

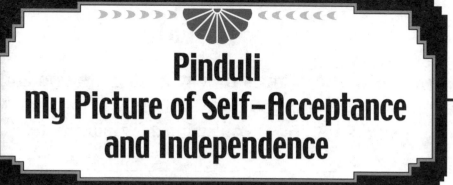

Pinduli
My Picture of Self-Acceptance and Independence

Activity #42: INDEPENDENCE

Fido

> "If you talk to the animals they will talk with you and you will know each other. If you do not talk to them you will not know them and what you do not know, you will fear. What one fears, one destroys."
>
> — Chief Dan George

Grades: K-5

Purpose: To provide a sense of independence
To provide the opportunity to take care of a living creature
To provide the opportunity to bond with another living creature

Materials: *To Bathe a Boa* by Imbior C. Kudrna (ISBN 0876144903)
List of possible pet options
Appropriate living space for pet chosen
Food for the pet
Water container if needed
Appropriate bedding
Important information about pet chosen

Procedures:
• Read *To Bathe a Boa.*
• Read list of possible pets.
• Discuss and vote on group pet.
• Research pets' needs.
• Make a list of all supplies needed.
• Buy pet and introduce it to group.
• Have the students decide on name for pet.
• Assign a "pet person of the week" for each of the weeks of group.
• Explain that the "pet person of the week" will be responsible for feeding, watering, and cleaning up after the pet.

Extension:
• Have the students write a story based on the class pet.
• Draw pictures of the pet.
• Have the students keep a pet diary.
• Have 1 student per weekend or holiday signed up to take pet home on the weekends and/or holidays. (Obtain parental permission first.)

Class Pet Possibilities

PET	SUPPLIES NEEDED
Rat	
Fish	
Mouse	
Bird	
Snake	
Hermit Crab	
Gerbil	
Ferret	
Lizard	
Ant Farm	
Turtle	
Rabbit	

Activity #43: INDEPENDENCE

Aqua World

> "Everything on the earth has a purpose,
> every disease an herb to cure it, and every person a mission.
> This is the Indian theory of existence"
>
> — Mourning Dove Salish

Grades: K-3

Purpose: To provide opportunity to see self as an individual and as part of a group
To provide the opportunity to be responsible for another living thing

Materials: "Grandmother River's Trick" from *When the Storm God Rides*
    by Florence Stratton
Fish Maze
Fish Template
Video of fish or pictures of brightly colored fish
Fish Tank Materials:
Fish Decoration Materials: Paint & Markers
                             Cardboard
                             Glitter & Buttons
                             Glue

Procedures: • Read "Grandmother River's Trick."
    Discuss: • What was Grandmother River's trick?
                  • What happened to the fish?
• Watch video of fish or look at pictures of brightly colored fish.
• Have the students sketch their favorite fish.
• Have students compare their sketches.
• Show the class pictures and descriptions of the fish from the pet store.
• Vote on which fish the class wants to purchase.
• Build the classroom aquarium.
• Introduce fish to its new home.
• Explain to students that it will be their responsibility to care for the fish.
• Have the students complete the fish maze.
• Have students complete the What I Like About Our Fish Work Sheet.
• Discuss how each fish is unique and individual but that the fish are part
  of a group called a "school."
• Kindergarten will need help with maze.

Extension: • Have the students decorate the fish template.
• Hang fish up from the ceiling.
• Make a costume out of the cardboard and decoration materials to look like
  their fish. Then they can put the costumes on and free dance around the
  room like the fish swimming in the aquarium.

What I Like About Our Fish

Colors	
Shape	
Movement	
What is the Purpose of Fish?	

Fish Maze

Start Here ↓

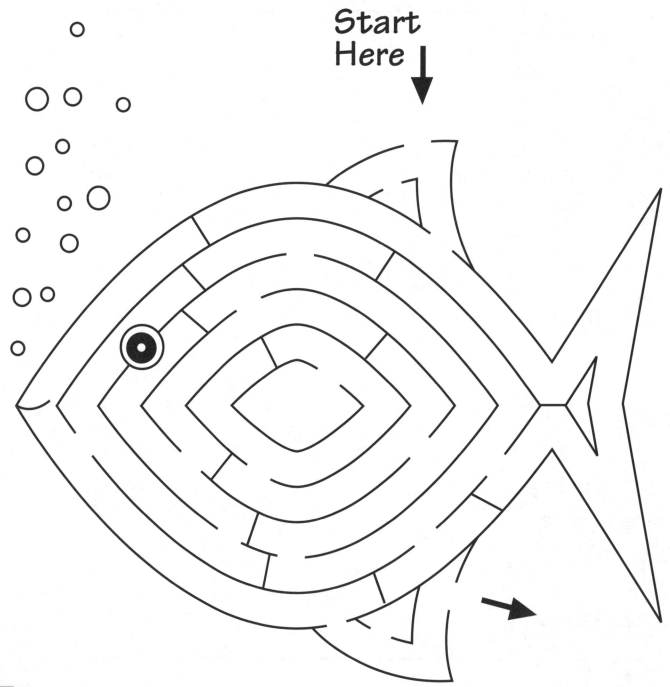

Grandmother River's Trick

From **When the Storm God Rides** Pages 87–90

Once the little fish that lived in a river, which was their grandmother, were in danger of being eaten by the garfish. The garfish, because they were long and slim, could catch the little fish without trouble. When the little fish fled through the water and tried to hide near the edges of banks and in shallow places of the river the long garfish darted after them, poked their slim snouts into the hiding places of the small fish and snapped them up in their sharp teeth. The hungry garfish were everywhere. They ate and ate but were never filled. They swam after the little fish day and night, churned up the river mud and gave the little fish no rest.

The little ones at last cried out to their grandmother, who was the river, to do something to help them. Grandmother River did not like the garfish, and she liked the little perch, the bass, and the minnows. She decided to play a trick on the big, hungry fish. She called to a big cloud that floated over her to send down some of its rain. The cloud heard. Twisting its dark, wet hair it sent down the rain in a great flood upon the river. As the rain began pouring into grandmother River she began to grow larger. She grew until she rose out of her banks and poured over the dry land. When the garfish saw what was happening they thought that here was a good chance to swim out upon the bushes and see if they could find something more they could eat. Instead of staying between the banks of the river with the little fish the garfish began to poke their noses into places where they had no business to be. They swam under the trees and the bushes and rolled their greedy eyes up at the grasshoppers and beetles.

And now Grandmother River played her trick. Quickly she gathered up her skirts to her knees and began running down to the sea, and as she ran she began dropping along her banks the dirt and sand she was carrying. Before the garfish saw what she was doing she had built up the banks higher than ever and had left them in little pools by themselves.

What a rage they were in when they saw how they had been fooled! They leaped in the air, they churned the pools, and they bit at one another. But it was no use. Grandmother River just gurgled along in her banks and the little fish played around as they pleased, happy to be safe from the sharp teeth ad hungry mouths of the garfish.

Activity #44: INDEPENDENCE
Courage of One

> "An Indian respects a brave man, but despises a coward.
> He loves a straight tongue, but hates a forked tongue."
> — Chief Joseph Nez Perce, 1879

Grades: 1-5

Purpose: To identify positive traits
To identify characteristics that we can respect in individuals

Materials: The book *Crazy Horse's Vision* by Joseph Bruchac (ISBN 1-880000-94-6)
My Hero/Heroine Is Worksheet
For My Hero/Heroine Worksheet
Me Being a Hero/Heroine Worksheet

Procedures: • Read *Crazy Horse's Vision.*
Discuss: • What is a hero/heroine?
• What does a hero/heroine look like?
• Who is your favorite hero/heroine?
• Could you be a hero/heroine?
• How?
• Fill out the My Hero/Heroine Is Worksheet

Extension: • Write a poem for your hero using the For My Hero/Heroine Worksheet.
• Draw a picture of how you could be a hero using the Me Being a
Hero/Heroine Worksheet.

My Hero/Heroine

My hero/heroine is

_____

Because

_____

_____

_____

Two words that describe my hero/heroine

_____

One interesting thing about my hero/heroine is

_____

One way I can be more of a hero/heroine is to

_____

For My Hero/Heroine

Dear _____,

You are my hero/heroine. This is a poem for you.

_____

_____

_____

_____

_____

_____

_____

_____

Respectfully,

_____

This is Me
Being a Hero/Heroine

Draw a picture of you being a hero/heroine.

Activity #45: INDEPENDENCE
Beautiful Dreamer

"The Person who has examined the nature of mind and relationships,
who purifies the energy of anger, avarice, envy, and fear and
who dedicates actions for the benefits of all beings,
such a person walks the beauty path."

— Dhyani Ywahoo

Grades: 4-6

Purpose: To teach students to think positively
To demonstrate that they are in charge of their thoughts, and that they
  can control them
To make students aware of positive and negative influences

Materials: Dream Catcher Legend
Dream Catcher directions
For each dream catcher you will need:
> Paper plate
> Yarn, any color
> Hole puncher
> Craft beads, feathers
> Markers, crayons, map pencils
> Scissors

Procedures:
• Read Dream Catcher legend to students.
  Discuss: • How do our thoughts affect our actions?
  • What kinds of positive and negative influences are around us?
  • How do they affect us? Our thoughts? Our actions?
• Invite students to create a dream catcher to place over their beds (or on
  chairs) to catch the positive thoughts, and release the negative thoughts.

Extension:
• With each bead that is placed on the dream catcher, label it with a positive
  influence in the student's life.
• Journal about positive and negative influences in life.
• How do these affect your thoughts and actions?
• What do you have within you that is a "dream-catcher" to filter out the
  negative thoughts and influences?

Dream Catcher Legend;
Lakota Dream Catcher History

Long ago an old Lakota spiritual leader was on a high mountain and had a vision. In his vision, Iktomi, the great trickster and searcher of wisdom, appeared in the form of a spider. As he spoke, Iktomi the spider picked up the elder's willow hoop, which had feathers, horsehair, beads and offerings on it, and began to spin a web. He spoke to the elder about the cycles of life, how we begin our lives as infants, move on through childhood and on to adulthood. Finally we go to old age where we must be taken care of as infants, completing the cycle. But, Iktomi said as he continued to spin his web, "In each time of life there are many forces, some good and some bad. If you listen to the good forces, they will steer you in the right direction. But, if you listen to the bad forces, they'll steer you in the wrong direction and may hurt you. So these forces can help, or can interfere with the harmony of Nature." While the spider spoke, he continued to weave his web.

When Iktomi finished speaking, he gave the elder the web and said, "The web is a perfect circle with a hole in the center. Use the web to help your people reach their goals, making good use of their ideas, dreams and visions. If you believe in the great spirit, the web will catch your good ideas and the bad ones will go through the hole.

The elder passed on his vision to the people and now many Indian people have a dream catcher above their bed to sift their dreams and visions. The good is captured in the web of life and carried with the people, but the evil in their dreams drops through the hole in the web and is no longer a part of their lives.

Make a Dream Catcher

SUPPLIES:

- Paper plate
- Hole puncher
- Markers, crayons, map pencils

- Yarn, any color
- Craft beads, feathers
- Scissors

INSTRUCTIONS:

- Begin by cutting out the center of the paper plate. Leave a rim of 2 inches around the paper plate.

- Using the hole punch, punch holes in the rim of the paper plate, about ? inch apart.

- Measure yarn 5-6 ft long. Tie one end of the yarn to any of the holes on the rim of the paper plate.

- Weave the yarn up, over, and all around the paper plate from one hole to the next. Be sure to loop through each of the punched holes.

- Add the craft beads to the middle of the dream catcher with the yarn as you go through the holes. Slip them onto the yarn and continue with the next hole. They will appear to be in the middle of the dream catcher.

- Once all of the holes are threaded with the yarn, tie a knot at the end of the yarn with the plate and the last hole.

- Punch 3 more holes in the paper plate at the bottom of the plate.

- Cut 3 more pieces of yarn, each about 5 inches long.

- Tie the yarn to the 3 punched holes at the bottom of the dream catcher.

- Choose some beads to thread onto each of the 3 yarn pieces and then tie one feather to the end each of the hanging yarn pieces.

- Using the markers, decorate the edges of the paper plate.

- Make a piece of yarn the length you need to hang it on the wall. Punch one more hole to the top of the paper plate dream catcher and tie the yarn to it.

Hang the Dream Catcher in a place where sweet thoughts are welcome.

Activity #46: INDEPENDENCE

I Am Unique!

> "The reason Wakan Tanka does not make two birds…or two human beings exactly alike is because each is placed here…to be an independent individual to rely on himself."
>
> — Okute

Grades: 1-6

Purpose: To help students realize their uniqueness.

Materials: *The Star Maiden* by Barbara Juster Esbensen and Helen K. Davie
(ISBN 0-316-24955-6)
Mirror (one big one for everyone to look at, or one for each student or pair)
Paint and paintbrushes or markers and colored pencils
Or camera and film
I Am Unique Worksheet

Procedures:
- Brainstorm: What does unique mean? What kinds of things are unique?
- Read *The Star Maiden.*
  - **Discuss:** • What made the Star Maiden unique?
    - What could she have chosen to be on earth?
    - What did she finally choose to be?
    - Invite students to look at their reflection in the mirror.
    - What makes them unique?
    - What sets them apart from everyone else?
- Disseminate paper, paint, and paintbrushes or markers and colored pencils.
- Invite students to paint their self-portrait or take their pictures with camera.
- Around their self-portrait, they should create images or symbols of what makes them unlike anyone else.
- Share.

Extension:
- Create an acrostic poem using student's name.
- Each line should describe something that is unique about the student.

I Am Unique

Activity #47: INDEPENDENCE

Go Fishing for Put-Ups

> "To clothe a man falsely is only to distress his spirit"
>
> — Standing Bear

Grades: 2-5

Purpose: Students will learn the difference between put-ups and put-downs

Students will learn how to think positively about self, and increase positive self-talk

Materials: "The Woodpecker's Stumpy Tail" from *When the Storm God Rides* by Florence Stratton

Fish Cutouts (several for each student)

Pencil, crayons, map pencils

Hole Punch

Pipe Cleaners

Scissors

Glue

Construction paper for fish cutouts

Procedures:
- Read "The Woodpecker's Stumpy Tail."
  - **Discuss:**
    - What was the old frog's warning
    - What was the reaction of the Indians and the woodpecker to the frog's warnings?
    - Do you think it hurt the frog's feelings when he was laughed at?
    - What was the reaction of the birds to the frog's warnings?
    - What happened to the woodpecker's tail?
    - Have you ever felt picked on like the fish picked on the woodpecker?
- Have students create a Fish Book with the Fish Cutouts.
- Each page in the book should start with: "I choose to remember this "put up" given to me rather than the "fish bites.""
- Students can use as many pages as they choose, but each page should list something the students are good at or a positive quality about themselves.
- Connect the book by punching holes at the mouth for the "stringer."
- Thread pipe cleaner through the holes to create the stringer.

Extension:
- Create a Bulletin Board of A Sea of Put-Ups swimming with the students' fish.

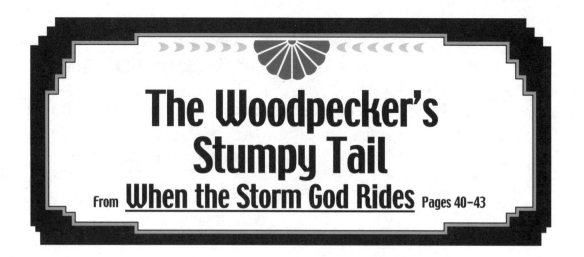

The Woodpecker's Stumpy Tail
From When the Storm God Rides Pages 40-43

The woodpecker, which knocks on the trees and cuts holes in them to find the bugs he eats, has a ragged, stumpy tail. He once had a long tail like other birds, but a fish bit part of it off.

It happened this way. Long ago a tribe of Indians lived in a country where floods often came in the spring and covered the earth and bushes with water. One spring a big flood was coming and only the frogs knew it. One old frog had lived close to the Indians so long that he could talk some of their language, and this old frog climbed upon a stump near the village where the Indians lived and warned them.

"Run for your lives? Flood's a-coming! Run for your lives! Flood's a –coming!" he boomed with his deep voice as he squatted on the stump.

Nobody paid any attention to him. The old frog puffed out his chest and boomed louder than before, "Run for your lives! Flood's a-coming! Run for your lives! Flood's a-coming!"

Now the Indians heard him and laughed at the old fellow. A woodpecker was sitting in a tree over his head, and he also began to laugh at the old frog. The other birds did not laugh, but flew out of the low trees and bushes and went to trees high enough to be above the flood when it came. The woodpecker kept on laughing and stayed with the foolish Indians by the bank of the river.

That night the rain began to pour down from the black sky. The river rose and rose. At last it tumbled over its bank and began running through the bushes and into the Indian village. The thunder boomed. The lightning cracked open the clouds. As the Indians jumped from their beds and began climbing into the trees the rain poured from the sky in sheets and the flood began rising over the boughs of the trees and washing the Indians away.

Now the woodpecker was frightened. He could not see to fly at night, and all he could do was to flutter from tree to tree hoping to find one high enough to be above the water. He perched on the very highest limb he could find, but even then his long black tail was hanging in the water running under him. As he was clinging to the limb and wishing he had listened to the old frog, a fish saw him there and made a snap at his tail. The lower end of it came off in the fish's sharp teeth. That is why the woodpecker has a short tail with jagged ends that look as if they had been bitten off.

Activity #48: INDEPENDENCE
When the Bugle Sounds

> "Chief Ross led in prayer and when the bugle sounded and the wagons started rolling many of the children waved their little hands goodbye to their mountain homes."
>
> — Private John Burnett

Grades: 4-6

Purpose: To help students cope with loss (moving, divorce, death, etc.)
To teach the value of ritual and ceremony

Materials: *Beyond the Ridge* by Paul Goble (ISBN 0-02-736581-6)
Crayons, fabric, stickers, markers, paint, magazines
Bugle Template

Procedures:
- Read *Beyond the Ridge.*
  - **Discuss:**
    - The family's experience of the death of the Grandmother and how the family found comfort in Nature.
    - The Native American use of ceremony to mark important events (Passing of the Peace Pipe, The Talking Stick, Dances).
    - What are some of our ceremonies which help us mark important life events?
- Sit in a circle in a quiet natural area.
- Students share their thoughts and feelings about their losses.
- When everyone has shared, encourage students to walk around and find a natural object that symbolizes their loss.
- Students come back to the group bringing their object if possible and share why their object reminds them of their loss.
- Remind students that even though the lost person is no longer with them, they will hold on to the memories just as they are holding the object in their hands or their minds.
- Discuss the ritual of the Bugle used by the soldiers…to signify important events such as taps (go to bed at night or at a funeral), reveli (get up in the morning), and "charge!" (when going into battle).
- On the Bugle Template students draw a picture representing their loss.

Extension:
- Encourage students to journal about their feelings regarding their loss.
- Invite students to draw or create something to help them get through their emotions.
- Students plan a ritual in memory of their loss such as writing letters and sending them up in a balloon, planting a flower, or building.

If I Could Play the Bugle, I Would Play Taps for. . .

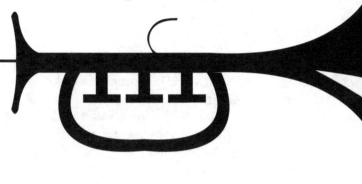

Draw a good-bye picture representing your loss.

CHAPTER 4
The Need for Generosity

Introduction

Native American youth prove their own virtue by helping other people. Power and purpose is demonstrated by contributing to others' lives. The group counselor can provide opportunities to build altruism, empathy and caring. Group exercises such at passing the talking stick gives the child the opportunity to share listening and talking time. After taking a nature walk during which "a stick finds the group," each member contributes to the decoration of the stick. This activity builds trust, cooperation and closeness within the group. The Gift exercise teaches the generosity of the Earth. The children are asked to search outside for "something special." This object may be anything that seems special to the child. The children bring their objects into the group, talk about it and why it has special qualities. The children are then reminded to always thank Mother Earth for sharing this special gift with them and the importance of environmental awareness.

Native American philosophy emphasizes that family includes animals, plants and minerals. This interrelatedness of all living beings is symbolized by the circle of life and is expressed in art and customs (Dufrene, 1990). The Native American practice of Give Away, as presented by McFadden (1999), can be used as a group activity to encourage children to honor others for their assistance and achievements and to promote the sharing of materials and self. The children are encouraged to make a token of their appreciation to another group member and to give it away as a demonstration that his/her efforts have been appreciated. With the use of pet therapy, children develop self-esteem when they give of themselves to animals that need care and love. The animals can be used as a vehicle to teach the art of sharing and taking turns, as each child in the group hands over the animal to the next child in line.

Sharing flowers or vegetables from the garden the children have planted and tended through the experience of nature therapy gives the child the opportunity to feel the intrinsic benefits of being generous and to receive the extrinsic reward of verbal praise for sharing. Animals and nature can provide the materials for projects involving volunteering. The collection of feathers, leaves and flowers can provide supplies for crafts to be made to share with others. Note cards, stationary, book covers and book marks made with the objects donated by Mother Earth make gifts to be presented to parents, teachers, peers and the elderly. The generosity of the animals and nature can be emphasized as the animals and earth provide gifts to the child who then shares the gifts with the people being visited. The children can plan an outing in which the counselor's pet is taken on visits to nursing homes or senior citizen centers. The Native American belief in the stewardship of nature can be emphasized as the children interact with nature and others who are in need.

Activity #49: GENEROSITY
Care for the Earth

> "The elders were wise. They knew that man's heart,
> away from nature, becomes hard; they knew that lack of respect
> for growing, living things,
> soon led to lack of respect for humans, too."
>
> — Chief Luther Standing Bear

Grades: 2-6

Purpose: To make connections among all living things and foster respect for them
To become aware of how we can improve our treatment of living things

Materials: "Why the Irises Hold Hands" from *When the Storm God Rides*
  by Florence Stratton
Easel Tablet
Markers
Caretaker of the Earth Contract
Caretakers of the Earth Affidavit Template
Large Poster Board
Blank Stickers
Scissors

Procedures:
- Read "Why the Irises Hold Hands."
  Discuss:
  - What clever things did the old tribe who lived along the coast of Texas know how to do?
  - What does it mean to "grow proud?"
  - What happened when these Indians began to forget about the Great Spirit who was so good to them and to think they could do every thing for themselves?
  - Instead of taking care of what they had been given, they caused the destruction of their lands.
  - Why were they given a second chance?
  - Of what is the wild iris to remind us?
- Students take turns going to the easel and drawing a picture of some way that people abuse any living thing, including other people.
- The student drawing does not tell the group what is being drawn.
- The group has to guess what the picture is showing (Pictionary game style).
- The person who calls out the correct answer first must then go to the easel and draw a picture that shows an "opposite" drawing of how the living thing could be cared for and treated in a respectful way.

Care for the Earth

> "The elders were wise. They knew that man's heart,
> away from nature, becomes hard; they knew that lack of respect
> for growing, living things,
> soon led to lack of respect for humans, too."
>
> — Chief Luther Standing Bear

Procedures:

- The person who calls out what that drawing is showing goes up and draws another situation of abuse or mistreatment, and so on.
- After everyone gets a few turns, students discuss their reactions to the examples of abuse and mistreatment that were drawn.
- Group makes an Affidavit of Care for the Earth.
- Contract with each student to take care of one living thing within the next week.
- Using the blank stickers, make seals of certification to be placed on the Contract.
- Conduct a ceremony planned and organized by the students.
- Each student signs own contract and the Affidavit decorated by the group.

Extension:

- Students journal about how much they appreciate living things in their environment and efforts they make to care for them.

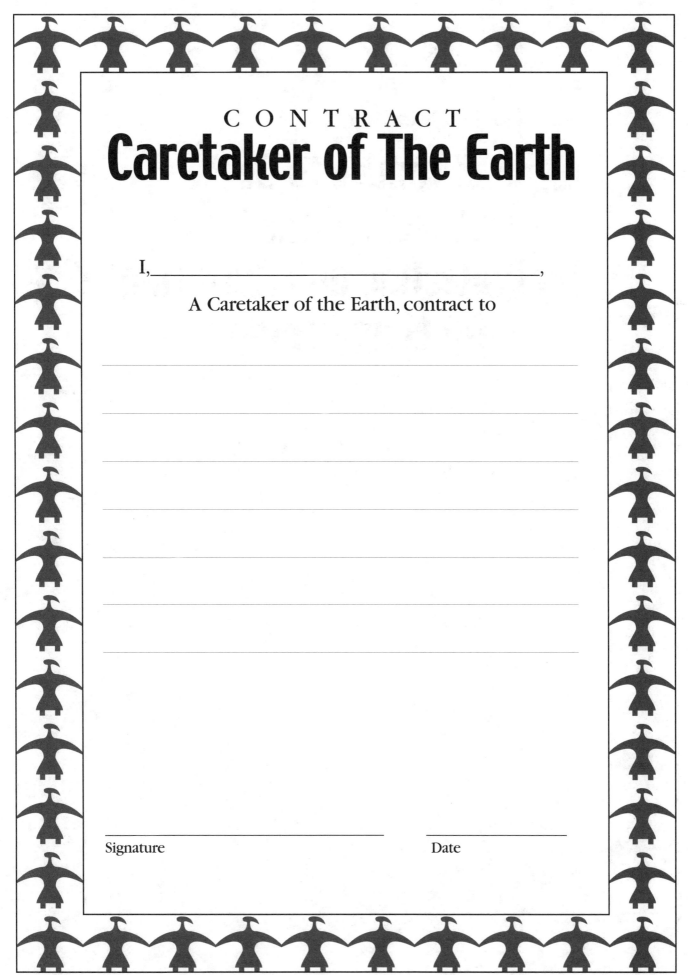

CONTRACT
Caretaker of The Earth

I,_____,

A Caretaker of the Earth, contract to

_____

_____

_____

_____

_____

_____

_____   _____
Signature   Date

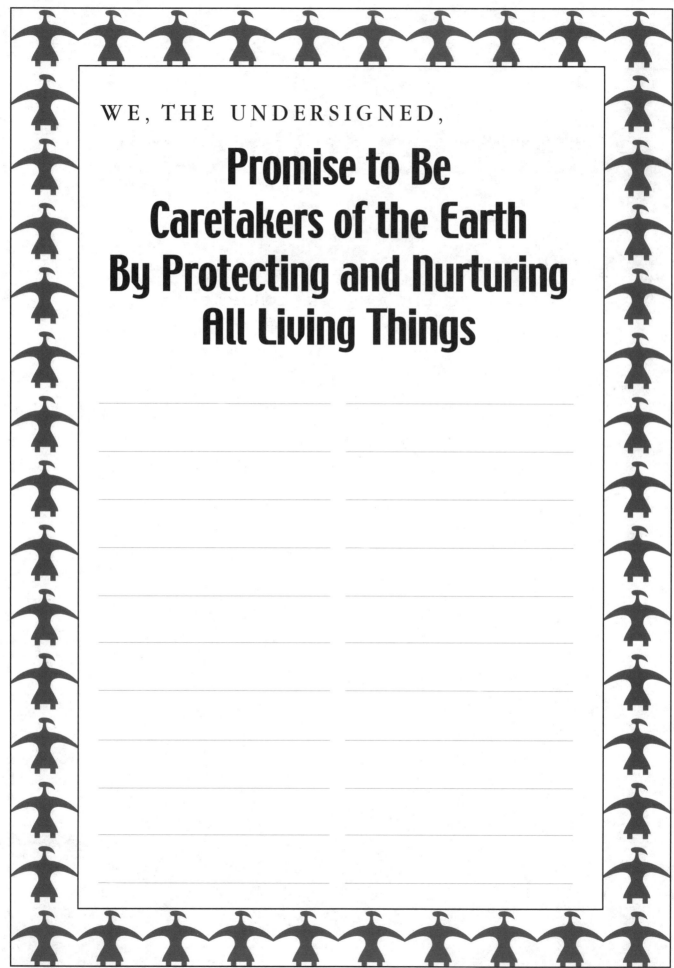

WE, THE UNDERSIGNED,

Promise to Be Caretakers of the Earth By Protecting and Nurturing All Living Things

Why the Irises Hold Hands

From **When the Storm God Rides** Pages 137–143

There is a pretty blue and purple flower with a heart of gold, which blooms in early spring in the swamps and along the streams of the gulf coast. It is called the blue flag or the wild iris. As long as it blooms it holds its head up as if looking for something. It seems to be waiting for something to happen. There is an old Indian legend that tells how this lovely flower came to be and why it lifts its head above the grasses around it.

There used to be along the coast of Texas a tribe of Indians who were more clever than any other Indian tribe had ever been. This tribe was an old one, and for many years the people had remembered what their fathers knew, and they taught the children all that the tribe had learned. Because of this the Indians knew how to do things no other tribes knew. They built large houses. They knew how to plant seeds in the soil and make them grow food. They knew how to paint on skins, carve bones and write the sign language.

Because these Indians were so clever the Great Spirit loved them very much. He would stretch himself out on a soft cloud high in the sky on summer days and look down on the Indians as they worked and played in their camp. Because he loved them he sent them gentle rains when their crops needed water. He made it easy for them to find birds and animals to eat. He answered their prayers.

But these Indians at last stopped praying. They began to forget about the Great Spirit who was so good to them, and to think they could do everything for themselves. They grew proud. They no longer looked toward the sky to talk with the Great Spirit, but began to look upon themselves as gods.

When the Great Spirit saw this he became very angry..........He decided to punish them. So it happened that while the people of the tribe were walking about their camp a great dark cloud came quickly over the sun in the blue sky, and the sky became black. Then the Great Spirit, who had sent the cloud, waited to see if this made the Indians afraid of him. They were not afraid, but went into their strong houses and laughed at the rain coming down. As the Great Spirit saw this he was more angry than ever. He decided to destroy the proud tribe.

He took a deep breath and blew strong winds across the Gulf of Mexico towards the camp. The clouds began to rush through the sky when he hurled them with his hands, and they hit each

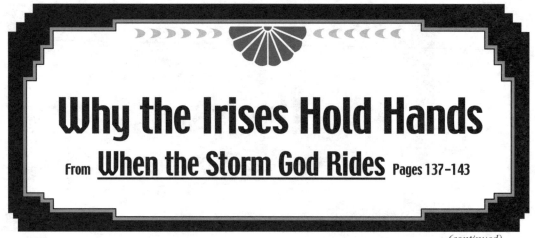

Why the Irises Hold Hands

From <u>When the Storm God Rides</u> Pages 137–143

(continued)

other and broke into sharp rain. He opened his mouth and shouted and out came thunder. Lightning darted from his angry eyes. . . . .

The water rose higher about their houses. At last they climbed to the roofs. Husbands and wives and children joined hands to die together. Still they did not cry out. Finally the rushing waters covered them all. Together they went down into the dark, rolling waves.

They were brave. As the Great Spirit saw this he thought that such people ought to have another chance to live. Perhaps they would become wiser and better if they lived again, so he decided that they could come alive when the last of the floodwaters had rolled back into the Gulf.

While they waited to be brought to life once more they should have the form of a new kind of plant. The Great Spirit decided this. He turned them into plants as they lay under water, and because they were in the water they grew roots, which could live in it and could live nowhere else. As they had died with their hands linked together they now took the form of plants with their roots linked together. When spring came the plants put forth blue flowers which lifted their heads to see if the last of the flood waters had rolled back into the Gulf so they could take the shape of people once more.

This is the way they grow to this day. We call them wild irises or flag lilies. They still grow in low and watery places. Their roots still cling together. Their heads are still listed, for they are waiting to see when the last of the waters return to the Gulf. Each year they find the marshes and low places still filled with water and so they must wait a while longer.

And this is the legend of the wild iris.

Activity #50: GENEROSITY
Natural Gifts

> "The survival of the world depends upon our sharing what we have and working together. If we don't, the whole world will die. First the planet, and next the people."
>
> — Fools Crow

Grades: 2-6

Purpose: To understand how to give valuable gifts that cannot be purchased
To become aware of the gifts we have within ourselves to give to others

Materials: "Kachina Brings the Spring" from *When the Storm God Rides*
  by Florence Stratton
The Giving Tree by Shel Silverstein
Natural Gifts Worksheet

Procedures:
- Read "Kachina Brings the Spring."
- Read *The Giving Tree.* (ISBN 0-06025665-6)
  Discuss:
  - What valuable gift did the little Indian girl give?
  - What valuable gifts did the tree give?
  - Have you received gifts that were not purchased?
  - How did you feel about receiving those gifts?
  - Have there been times when you have given gifts, which were not purchased?
  - Have you given of yourself as the tree gave of itself?
  - How did you feel about those gifts you gave?
    own contract and the Affidavit decorated by the group.
- The Natural Gifts Worksheet is discussed giving examples of gifts of patience, humor, etc.
- Students complete the Natural Gifts Worksheet.

Extension:
- Students create a project to help the elderly in a nursing home.
- The requirements for the project are that the gifts should not be tangible and only transportation to the nursing home is needed.
- Project ideas: Reading books to the residents
  Singing songs
  Putting on skits
  Playing board games

Natural Gifts Worksheet

Rank the following gifts in order of what you would like to give to others.
Next to each, explain how you could give these gifts of yourself to other people.

Time	**Humor**
Understanding	**Forgiveness**
Patience	**Acceptance**
Love	**Physical strength**

1. _____

2. _____

3. _____

4. _____

5. _____

6. _____

7. _____

8. _____

Kachina Brings the Spring

From <u>When the Storm God Rides</u> Pages 15–25

An Indian tribe living in the southwestern country was once filled with fear and suffering. It was the beginning of spring, when the green buds should have been peeping from the trees, and new flowers should have been lifting their fresh, cheery faces from the grass, but something was wrong with this springtime. It was not like spring. There was no rain from the hard blue skies that looked down without tears of pity on the hills and prairies that would not flower and the dry creek beds where water used to flow. And the weather should have been warm, but it was bitter cold. In the day the sun was far away and had no heat. In the night the moon and stars were like cold steel in the wide, black sky, where no clouds floated.

Because of these things the Indians suffered great hunger. There was little food, only parched corn and acorns and shreds of dried buffalo meat. The animals and birds, which the Indians used to shoot and eat, could not live there without water and food, and they had died or had left the country. The berries that the tribe needed to eat could not grow in the dry earth. There was no rain to call them up from their sleep under the ground.

The Indians could not find food and began to starve. Women and children grew weak. One night the tribe's medicine man, the wrinkled, wise old Indian who knew how to get good spirits to grant the Indians' wishes, came out of his wigwam and beat loudly on his drum. He was calling the tribe to come to listen to him. The Indians hurried around him and watched as he pounded on his drum and danced and shouted a song.

Suddenly the medicine man cried to the Indians, "Ho! Hear me! The Great Spirit has thundered in my ears and told me to speak. He has taken away from us the rain and the flowers and the animals because we have angered him. But he will give us help if we will make him a burnt offering. We must burn something, which we love most and gather its ashes and scatter them to the four winds of heaven. Then the winds will carry the ashes to the Great Spirit and he will be pleased again. Go back to your wigwams and think what we love most. Tomorrow we will burn it when the sun rises."

Among the Indians who listened to the medicine man was a little girl. She was holding in her thin arms a wonderful kachina doll made for her by her grandmother. This kachina was far prettier than any of the others in the tribe. It was made of wood carved with a flint knife. Painted on the wooden form were the clothes of a warrior, an Indian brave. On its head was a war bonnet of blue feathers and its eyes were made of two little black beads dyed from berries. The little Indian maiden loved her kachina, carried it with her when she played and slept with it in her arms at night.

When this little girl heard what the Great Spirit wanted she almost cried, for she felt in her heart that nothing among her people was more loved than her own doll. But she looked up and saw the shadows of pain in the face of her hungry mother. She saw how thin was the face of her baby brother strapped to his mother's back in his cradle. She looked down at

Kachina Brings the Spring

From <u>When the Storm God Rides</u> Pages 15–25

(continued)

her beloved little doll, held it tightly to her breast and slipped away to her father's wigwam where she lay for a long time with her face pressed close against her doll.

The lodges were still and the fire in the middle of the camp had died down to red embers when the little girl came out again. In her arms was her doll. She knew she loved her kachina more than anything else was loved in the tribe, and she had decided to give it up as the Great Spirit had asked, so that her people would be happy again.

She cried a little bit as she laid twigs on the dying embers of the fire. But she blew the fire until it sprang up into a blaze that made the shiny eyes of her doll sparkle, so they seemed to be bright with tears, like her own. She hugged the doll and kissed it. Now she laid it in the middle of the flames. Quickly the flames began to eat the doll. The blue feathers on its head were gone, the tiny shoes turned into smoke, the beady eyes fell off the face into the fire, and soon there was nothing left of the doll the little girl had loved.

Now she raked out the ashes and sat down to watch them cool. When they had cooled she took them in her two hands and held them up while the cool wind blew them out of her hands and into the darkness. Finally the little girl stooped and patted the ground where the ashes of her doll had lain. Then a wonderful thing happened. Where the ground was bare and hard before, it was now covered with soft leaves that felt warm to her cold little hands. The sharp cold of the night wind now was gone, and the smell of spring flowers seemed to fill the air around her. The Great Spirit must have been pleased with the offering of her doll. Happy once more, the little girl hurried to her wigwam and lay down to sleep.

In the morning the child was awakened with the sound of joyous cries outside. She heard drums beating and heard dancing feet. The Indians were singing. She peeped outside and saw that she had pleased the Great Spirit, because for the first time in many moons a misty rain was falling, a rain that was good to the thirsty earth. The cold wind was gone, too. The warm south wind was gently blowing through the rain and rustling trees that were heavy with new green leaves. Everywhere the hills and prairies were covered with strange and lovely flowers the Indians had never seen before. When she ran to pick one of them she saw that they were shaped like the bonnet of feathers her doll had worn, and blue like those feathers. At the heart of each small blossom was a speck of red, just like the red of the fire, which had burned her doll. And the tips of buds were silver gray, like the ashes that were left after it had burned.

When the little girl hurried with one of the new flowers to the Indians they knew what had happened. She had given her doll to the Great Spirit and he had given back to her millions of flowers that were now lying on the hills like a piece of blue sky fallen to earth. And spring had come at last. The Indians named the new flowers blue bonnets, because they were like the blue bonnet of the little girl's doll. Today, when the bluebonnets appear on the Texas prairies, it is a sign that the Great Spirit has once more returned springtime to the earth.

Activity #51: GENEROSITY
Little Cloud and Wild Flowers

> "We once gave you our hearts. You now have them."
>
> — Satank

Grades: 2-6

Purpose: To teach that we can be generous through our actions with others
To provide opportunity to realize that generosity can enrich the lives of others

Materials: "The Cloud That Was Lost" from *When the Storm God Rides*
  by Florence Stratton
Giving of Myself Drawing Sheet
Crayons, Markers, Map Pencils

Procedures:
- Read "The Cloud That Was Lost."
  Discuss:
  - Why are the clouds glad when the sun goes down?
  - Why do people see white clouds on the mountaintops?
  - How did the little cloud get lost?
  - How did we know the little cloud was crying?
  - Where did the little cloud sleep?
  - What color were the flowers where the cloud was sleeping?
  - What color were the flowers after they opened their mouths and drank in the little cloud?
  - The wild phlox flowers were changed to beautiful pink and lavender colors because the little cloud gave of himself.
  - When we give of ourselves by doing generous things we change the lives of others.
- Students draw a picture showing a time in their lives that they extended themselves to help someone else.
- Students share their pictures and experiences with the group.
- Discuss how it feels to help others.

Extension:
- Have group members brainstorm ways to be helpful and to give things to people without spending money.
- Display the pictures in the room for a week, then send the pictures home with the students as a reminder to help others

Giving of Myself

Draw a picture of a time when you helped someone else.

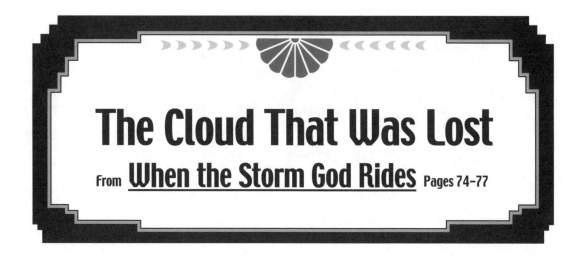

The Cloud That Was Lost

From **When the Storm God Rides** Pages 74–77

In the country of high mountains the little white clouds that float around in the sky during the day go to sleep on the tops of the peaks. They do this because they become tired while waiting in the sky to grow heavy enough to send down the rains. All day the wind blows them this way and that, they bump into one another, and the sun makes them hot. Because of this they are glad when the sun at last goes down, for then they can float gently down to the mountain tops and curl themselves up among the trees and rest there until next morning. This is why people can see white clouds like fog on the mountains at night and at dawn.

Late one afternoon one little cloud had sailed off from its brothers and sisters. It had been chasing its tiny white tail like a puppy, had whirled and whirled head over heels until it was far away from the others. At last, when it was time to go to bed on the mountaintops, and all the other clouds were gone from the sky, the little cloud found itself all alone over a broad, flat land. It looked for the mountains but could not see them. The little cloud was lost. The sun was down and it was time to go to bed, but there were no mountains to be seen. A few drops of rain fell from the little lost cloud because it was crying.

After a while, just as the day was gone, the cloud was so sleepy it floated down and stretched itself out on the flat country, all by itself. Under it, where it was lying on the ground, were some sweet scented, white flowers. These flowers were tired of being white. They had long hoped to find some way to color themselves. Now the little sleeping cloud was colored light pink and lavender, and when the flowers felt the cloud float down upon them they opened their eyes and saw the lovely colors. They opened their throats and began to drink in the little cloud. They drank and they drank until at last the little cloud was all gone.

When morning came nothing was there but the flowers. Some were still white, but those that had drunk in the cloud were now pink and lavender, as the cloud had been. This is how the flowers called the wild phlox got their soft colors that look like the evening clouds.

Activity #52: GENEROSITY

Sacrifice of Love

> "Humankind has not woven the web of life. We are but one thread within it. Whatever we do to the web, we do ourselves. All things are bound together. All things connect."
>
> — Chief Seattle

Grades: 2-6

Purpose: To increase self-awareness and how to make sacrifices to help others
To promote positive actions toward helping others

Materials: *The Legend of the Bluebonnet* by Tomie DePaola (ISBN# 0-698-11359-4)
Sacrifice of Love Action Plan Letter
Sacrifice of Love Weekly Report

Procedures:
- Read *The Legend of the Bluebonnet* by Tomie DePaola.
  - **Discuss:**
    - What does it mean to make a sacrifice?
    - Has there been a time in your lives when you may have had to make a sacrifice to help others (such as giving up TV time to help with a house hold chore)?
    - How do you think the girl felt about giving up her only doll?
    - Do you think it was worth it?
- On the Sacrifice of Love Action Plan members will write a letter to their family telling them something they will do to help out at home.
(Ex: rinse dishes after dinner)

Extension:
- Have students journal throughout the next week on the Sacrifice of Love
- Weekly Report the sacrifices they made and how it helped others.
- During the next session acknowledge efforts made by group members and discuss with the members how it felt to them to help out.

Sacrifice of Love Plan

*Make an action plan below of how you are going
to be a more helpful member of your family.*

Dear_____,

I plan to give of myself in order to become a more
helpful member of my family. I plan to . . .

_____

_____

_____

_____

_____

_____

_____

Sincerely,

_____
Date

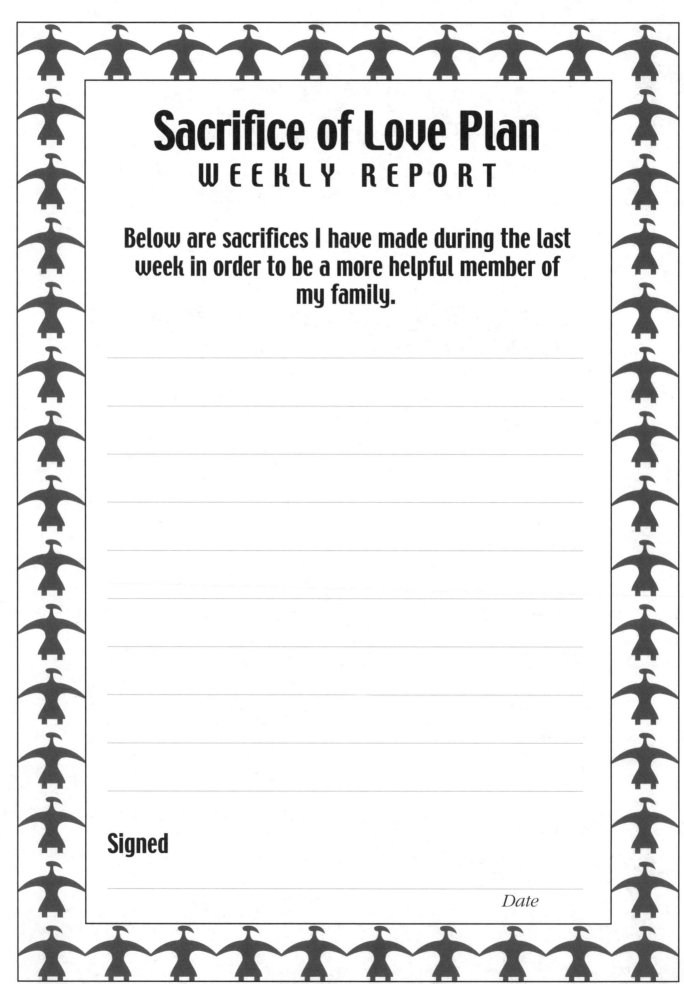

Sacrifice of Love Plan
WEEKLY REPORT

Below are sacrifices I have made during the last week in order to be a more helpful member of my family.

_____

_____

_____

_____

_____

_____

_____

_____

Signed

_____
Date

Activity #53: GENEROSITY
Light in Our Lives

> "We return our thanks to the moon and the stars,
> which have given us their light when the sun was gone."
>
> — Iriquois

Grades: 3-6

Purpose: To develop appreciation for those people who help students
To provide opportunity to show appreciation to these people

Materials: "When the Stars Took Root" from *When The Storm God Rides*
   by Florence Stratton
Pen or Pencil
Stationery
Light of My Life Thank You Worksheet

Procedures: • Read "When the Stars Took Root"
   Discuss: • Why did the daughter of the moon tribe want to live on earth?
      • How did she get there?
      • When it was time for her to return to the moon, what did she do?
      • The stars she threw down to earth which then became flowers are like the nice things you do for people. Those things help people feel better and then they help others in turn….like the stars turning into flowers and the flowers growing and growing.
      • What is the meaning of the phrase "light of my life?"
      • Compare traditional customs of giving such as birthday presents, Christmas presents etc. with giving of appreciation.
      • What does it mean to appreciate someone?
      • Whom do you appreciate in your lives?
   • Counselor shows the group the format for writing a thank you letter.
   • Group members pick a person who they appreciate and write them a thank you letter.
   • Allow group members to share whom they chose and why they are thanking them.
   • Write Thank You letters or draw Thank You pictures using the Light of My Life Thank You Template

Extension: • If possible, mail or deliver the letters.

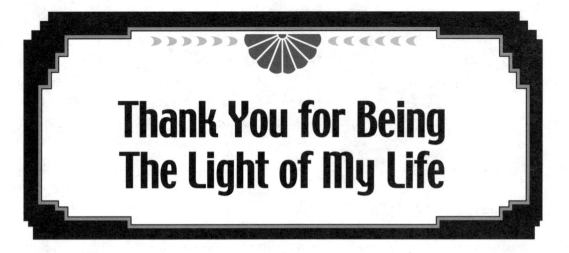

Thank You for Being
The Light of My Life

When the Stars Took Root

From **When the Storm God Rides** Pages 95–108

White men teach that the moon is a dead, empty world. Yet there was a time, says an Indian legend, when a tribe of Indians lived and hunted there. The chief of that tribe had a lovely daughter who at one time visited the earth and who flung down from the sky, after she had returned to her father's home on the moon, a handful of bright little stars which took root and grew as flowers. She did this because she loved the son of a chief on the earth.........

The daughter of the moon chief wanted to visit the earth and convinced an old witch who lived in a cave to help her go there. The old woman took up a bright magic blanket and wound it about the girl's shoulders, and as she did this the girl forgot all her life up to that moment. Now the witch drew from her robe an Indian flute made from a bone. She placed it to her dry lips and blew once, then again, then a third time. As the dying note of the flute was fading out in the depths of the cave the still air was suddenly filled with a rushing sound. With the speed of the wind a large eagle sailed into the cave, lit at the feet of the old woman and stood before her with his great wings still outstretched. The old woman told the eagle to fly to the earth with the young girl in his strong claws. The eagle obeyed. Out of the cave rushed the bird with the chief's daughter. Up above the white trees he rose, while his great wings roared as they beat the air. Soon they were far above the forest and flying as fast as the lightning towards the distant earth.

When the chief's daughter at last opened her eyes she was lying alone on the shores of an ocean. The eagle and the magic blanket were gone. But she was happy for she knew that she was now on earth. The girl walked along the ocean listening to the strange sound of the waves and gazing at the flowers she had never seen before. It was not long before she came upon a camp of Indians near the shore where she fell in love with the chief's son. They got married and all the tribe was happy, because the people liked them both. The women made the young man and his bride a large new wigwam painted all over with birds and animals and they made the bride some pots and bowls of clay. The two young people made their home and were happy with each other.

Just before the next spring came the daughter of the moon chief had a dream. She had it the next night, and the next after that. She knew what it meant. She knew that the time had come, as the old witch had told her, for her to go back to her father's home on the Moon.

155

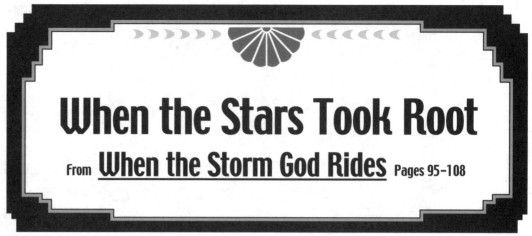
(continued)

When morning came the girl did not open her eyes. Her hands were cold. Her husband bent over her and saw that life had slipped out of her during the night. He knew that her dream had come true and that she has returned to the moon.

That night the husband sat near her grave by himself.

The waves of the gulf made the only sound that broke the stillness. Suddenly something made him raise his head and look up into the sky. He could see for an instant the misty shape of the one he loved, clad in the long robes in which she had been buried. She seemed to be made of the light that came from the stars. As he watched her she moved her hand and a shower of little stars began to fall towards him. Then he knew that the chief's daughter was on the way to her father on the moon and that she had thrown the stars down to him to let him know that she had not forgotten him.

Full of happiness the young man fell into a deep sleep and did not wake till morning had come to drive the stars from the sky. But morning had not driven them all away. All around his feet on the grass were hundreds of little flowers shaped like stars shining with the fresh dew. Some were white. Others were pink. Some had five pointed petals and some had six, but all had little hearts of gold. These were the stars that the daughter of the moon chief had thrown down to her husband as she left the earth. . . . .

Soon after that the young man was killed in battle. The people of his tribe laid him to rest by the side of his wife, and it was not long before the graves of both were covered with the little pink and white starflowers that can be found on the prairies today. The moon chief's daughter had thrown them down to tell the Indians that her husband had come up to her.

Activity #54: GENEROSITY
Use Your Gifts

> "A big man gives away what he has and shares with others."
> — New Guinea Elder

Grades: 3-6

Purpose: To use the gifts we naturally possess to help others.

Materials: *The Legend of the Indian Paint Brush* by Tomie dePaola
   (ISBN#0-698-11360)
Paper
Pen or Pencil
My Natural Gifts Chart
Using My Gifts Contract

Procedures: • Read *The Legend of the Paintbrush.*
   Discuss: • How did the young boy use his gifts to help others?
      • Natural gifts are abilities such as singing or artistic ability, caring, kindness, etc.
      • What natural gifts do you possess?
• Members will complete the My Natural Gifts Chart and think of ways to use their gifts to help others.
• Once group members have completed the chart allow them to share the results with the entire group.
• Contract with group members to use a specific natural gift with a specific person during the following week
• Fill out the Using My Gifts Contract

Extension: • Challenge the group to use their natural gifts to help someone over the next week.
• During the next session allow members to report on what they did.

My Natural Gifts

What gifts I possess	How I can use my gifts to help others

C O N T R A C T
My Natural Gifts

I,_____,

contract to use my Natural Gift of

_____

To help

_____

during the coming week.

_____   _____
Signature   Date

Activity #55: GENEROSITY
Grandmother River

> "Treat every person, from the tiniest child to the eldest elder, with respect at all times."
>
> — Cherokee Saying

Grades: 3-6

Purpose: To create a positive atmosphere by committing acts of kindness
To foster a sense of generosity and kindness in students
To provide opportunity to respond with kindness instead of cruelty

Materials: "Grandmother River's Trick" from *When The Storm God Rides*
by Florence Stratton
Fishing For Kindness Cards

Procedures:
• Read "Grandmother Rivers' Trick"
  Discuss:
  • Who was eating the little fish?
  • What did grandmother River do to trick the garfish?
  • How did Grandmother River's one act of kindness help lots of little fish?
  • How do you think the little fish felt about her kindness?
  • What are ways we can get rid of the garfish (negative words and behavior) to help the little fish (other people) in our school)?
• Divide students into groups of four.
• Pass out Fishing for Kindness Cards.
• Send groups out into the school to "go fishing" for opportunities to be kind in the next 10-15 minutes.
• When students come back, discuss how they felt about their "fishing trip" during which they were kind to some one.

Extension:
• Track Acts of kindness from the original fishing expedition."
• Try to determine if the school atmosphere has changed into a more positive, kind atmosphere.
• Create a Fishing for Kindness club at school that anonymously commits acts of kindness throughout the school.

160

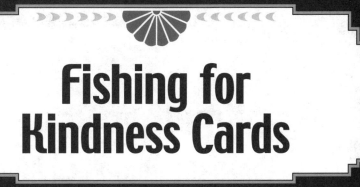

Fishing for Kindness Cards

It's Your Turn!
Go do something good
for some one else.
Do it anonymously.
Pass on this card.

It's Your Turn!
Go do something good
for some one else.
Do it anonymously.
Pass on this card.

It's Your Turn!
Go do something good
for some one else.
Do it anonymously.
Pass on this card.

Grandmother River's Trick
From <u>When the Storm God Rides</u> Pages 87–90

Once the little fish that lived in a river, which was their grandmother, were in danger of being eaten by the garfish. The garfish, because they were long and slim, could catch the little fish without trouble. When the little fish fled through the water and tried to hide near the edges of banks and in shallow places of the river the long garfish darted after them, poked their slim snouts into the hiding places of the small fish and snapped them up in their sharp teeth. The hungry garfish were everywhere. They ate and ate but were never filled. They swam after the little fish day and night, churned up the river mud and gave the little fish no rest.

The little ones at last cried out to their grandmother, who was the river, to do something to help them. Grandmother River did not like the garfish, and she liked the little perch, the bass, and the minnows. She decided to play a trick on the big, hungry fish. She called to a big cloud that floated over her to send down some of its rain. The cloud heard. Twisting its dark, wet hair it sent down the rain in a great flood upon the river. As the rain began pouring into grandmother River she began to grow larger. She grew until she rose out of her banks and poured over the dry land. When the garfish saw what was happening they thought that here was a good chance to swim out upon the bushes and see if they could find something more they could eat. Instead of staying between the banks of the river with the little fish the garfish began to poke their noses into places where they had no business to be. They swam under the trees and the bushes and rolled their greedy eyes up at the grasshoppers and beetles.

And now Grandmother River played her trick. Quickly she gathered up her skirts to her knees and began running down to the sea, and as she ran she began dropping along her banks the dirt and sand she was carrying. Before the garfish saw what she was doing she had built up the banks higher than ever and had left them in little pools by themselves.

What a rage they were in when they saw how they had been fooled! They leaped in the air, they churned the pools, and they bit at one another. But it was no use. Grandmother River just gurgled along in her banks and the little fish played around as they pleased, happy to be safe from the sharp teeth ad hungry mouths of the garfish.

Activity #56: GENEROSITY

The Gift of You

> "The color of the skin makes no difference; what is good and just for one is good and just for the other."
>
> — White Shield, Arikara

Grades: 1-5

Purpose: To understand the value of sharing with others
To discuss the importance of being a good friend

Materials: *The Rainbow Fish* by Marcus Pfister ISBN# 1-55858-009-3
Fish Template
Crayons or Markers
Aluminum foil

Procedures:
- Read the story *The Rainbow Fish*.
  - **Discuss:**
    - How did the Rainbow Fish feel before he gave away his special scales?
    - How did the Rainbow Fish feel after he gave away his special scales?
- Have each student decorate his or her own rainbow fish.
- They are to use the aluminum foil to symbolize their special scale or qualities.
- Then ask each student to discuss what he or she would share with others if they were asked.

Extension:
- Role-play real life situations where you can share in order to help others.
- Brainstorm a list of characteristics that each student can share with others.
- Homework: Each student will identify one trait that they can share with others this week.

Activity #57: GENEROSITY
The Gift of the Turtle

> "One never forgets to acknowledge a favor, no matter how small."
> — Moral Teaching of the Omaha

Grades: 2-5

Purpose: To gain an appreciation of giving and receiving
To strengthen the bond with nature

Materials: *Thirteen Moons on A Turtle's Back* by Joseph Bruchac
(ISBN # 0-698-11584-8)
Thirteen Gifts Worksheet

Procedures:
- Read *Thirteen Moons on a Turtle's Back.*
  Discuss: • The 13 gifts and celebrations.
  • What other gifts does nature share with us?
- Students complete the Thirteen Gifts Worksheet by writing on each scale a gift that they could give to nature or others.

Extension:
- Each student will find a gift from nature to give to someone else in the group.
- Ask the students to focus on the appreciation of receiving the gift.

The Thirteen Gifts Worksheet

Write on each scale a gift that you can give to nature or others.

Activity #58: GENEROSITY
Sunshine or Shadows

> "I hear nothing but pleasant words."
>
> — Mongazid (1825)

Grades: 3-5

Purpose: To learn to change negative self-talk into positive self-talk
To learn to be generous to others by what we say to them
To learn to be generous to ourselves by what we say to ourselves

Materials: "When the Rainbow Was Torn" from *When the Storm God Rides*
  by Florence Stratton
Digital or Polaroid camera/film OR individual pictures of students
Rays of Sunshine Template
Markers
Tape or glue

Procedures:
- Read "When the Rainbow Was Torn."
  - **Discuss:**
    - What did the cactus do to change its flowers from white to red and orange and yellow?
    - It chose to reach for the colors in the light of the rainbow in order to be colorful and happy.
    - Standing in the sunshine can warm our bodies and our feelings.
    - By the same token, choosing to think positive thoughts can make us feel warmly (positively) about our selves.
    - We can choose to stand in the sunshine (think positive thoughts).
    - Or we can choose to stand in the shadows (think negatively about our selves or others.)
- Take picture of each student
- Tape or glue the picture to the top of construction paper.
- Have student write their name at the top of their page.
- Invite students to go around and write "Rays of Sunshine" (something positive about their classmates) on their sheets.
  - Something they like about that person
  - Something nice they remember about the person
- Everyone MUST write something nice on everyone else's page.
- When finished, invite students to read their pages.
  - **Discuss:**
    - How does it feel to find out that people think good things about you?
    - How did it feel to spread "Rays of Sunshine?"
- Encourage students to keep their pages with them to refer to whenever they are feeling a little down on themselves.

Extension:
- Continue this activity throughout the year by creating student "mail boxes" out of shoeboxes or paper bags.
- Students should decorate boxes/bags however they'd like.
- Invite class to anonymously place "rays of sunshine"/positive comments in the mailboxes.

Rays of Sunshine

When the Rainbow Was Torn
From <u>When the Storm God Rides</u> Pages 152–155

There are flowers whose petals have in them part of the very colors belonging to the rainbow. These are the cactus flowers, the blooms that burst out like orange, red or yellow flame from the tips of the thorny cactus plants. It used to be that all these flowers were white, as some are now. But one day the rainbow gave most of them colors that they have kept up to this time.

The white cactus flowers used to turn up their faces and look at the bright bow that arched across the sky whenever the sun shone through the rain or mist. The two ends of the rainbow always touched the earth somewhere, and where they touched everything on the ground seemed to be washed in the rainbow's colors. But the rainbow had never touched the cactus plants. Perhaps it was afraid of the sharp thorns that grew on them. The white cactus flowers always hoped that some day they would be bathed in misty colors. Yet the rainbow would never come near them.

Once after a heavy rain the rainbow was up in the sky getting ready to send its two ends down to earth. The rainbow itself was heavy with raindrops. As its ends sank down it took care not to let them fall upon the thorns of the cactus plants. But, just as one of the ends was about to dip to the ground the rainbow suddenly saw a bed of cactus plants hidden in a little cluster of high grass. When it saw the plants the rainbow tried to lift its end again, but the end was so heavy with the raindrops that it kept sinking down, and at last it brushed across the cactus plants with their white flowers.

When this happened the thorns caught at the misty bands of colors to try to keep them for the flowers. The violet, indigo, blue and green bands slipped out of their way, but the yellow, red and orange bands became hung on the thorns. Just as soon as this happened the happy cactus flowers opened their petals wide and began to drink in the colored mists that were clinging to the plants. Before the rainbow had pulled itself loose from the thorns the white flowers had filled themselves with the colors and were now red and orange and yellow themselves.

Activity #59: GENEROSITY
Kindness Counts

> "As a child I understood how to give; I have forgotten this grace
> since I became civilized."
> — Ohiyesa

Grades: 3-5

Purpose: To teach the difference between kind and unkind behavior
To provide the opportunity to focus attention on kind behavior

Materials: "Kachina Brings the Spring" from *When the Storm God Rides*
   by Johnson and Chute
Chart paper
Kindness Counts Worksheet
Puppets
Catching Kindness Worksheet

Procedures:
- Read "Kachina Brings the Spring."
  - **Discuss:**
    - What does kindness mean?
    - What was the problem in the Indian Village?
    - What kind thing did the little girl do to help the Village?
    - Was it easy for her to do?
    - What happened as a result of her kindness?
    - Brainstorm ways to be kind and unkind to others.
- Have students (in pairs) create a role-play (using themselves or puppets) depicting a kind act and an unkind act.
- Discuss each role-play as a class.
- Complete Kindness Counts Worksheet

Extension:
- Have students look through newspapers and magazines to find examples of kindness.
- Make a Kindness Collage.
- Challenge students to "Catch Kindness" by observing other doing kind things for each other.
- Draw pictures of their observations of kind behavior on the Catch Kindness Template or take pictures with a camera.
- Post pictures on bulletin board.

Kindness Counts

Name _____ Date _____

Everyday people show their kindness to us. Sometimes we realize it, and sometimes we don't. In the space below, draw a picture of someone being kind to another.

Has there been a time when you have been kind to someone or they have been kind to you? Draw a picture and write a short paragraph about it.

_____

_____

_____

_____

Catching Kindness

Below is a drawing or picture of Kind Behavior.

Kachina Brings the Spring

From <u>When the Storm God Rides</u> Pages 15–25

An Indian tribe living in the southwestern country was once filled with fear and suffering. It was the beginning of spring, when the green buds should have been peeping from the trees, and new flowers should have been lifting their fresh, cheery faces from the grass, but something was wrong with this springtime. It was not like spring. There was no rain from the hard blue skies that looked down without tears of pity on the hills and prairies that would not flower and the dry creek beds where water used to flow. And the weather should have been warm, but it was bitter cold. In the day the sun was far away and had no heat. In the night the moon and stars were like cold steel in the wide, black sky, where no clouds floated. And because of these things the Indians suffered great hunger. There was little food, only parched corn and acorns and shreds of dried buffalo meat. The animals and birds, which the Indians used to shoot and eat, could not live there without water and food, and they had died or had left the country. And the berries that the tribe needed to eat could not grow in the dry, hard earth. There was no rain to call them up from their sleep under the ground. The Indians could not find food and began to starve. Women and children grew weak. One night the tribe's medicine man, the wrinkled, wise old Indian who knew how to get good spirits to grant the Indians' wishes, came out of his wigwam and beat loudly on his drum. He was calling the tribe to come to listen to him. The Indians hurried around him and watched as he pounded on his drum and danced and shouted a song.

Suddenly the medicine man cried to the Indians, "Ho! Hear me! The Great Spirit has thundered in my ears and told me to speak. He has taken away from us the rain and the flowers and the animals because we have angered him. But he will give us help if we will make him a burnt offering. We must burn something, which we love most and gather its ashes and scatter them to the four winds of heaven. Then the winds will carry the ashes to the Great Spirit and he will be pleased again. Go back to your wigwams and think what we love most. Tomorrow we will burn it when the sun rises."

Among the Indians who listened to the medicine man was a little girl. She was holding in her thin arms a wonderful kachina doll made for her by her grandmother. This kachina was far prettier than any of the others in the tribe. It was made of wood carved with a flint knife. Painted on the wooden form were the clothes of a warrior, an Indian brave. On its head was a war bonnet of blue feathers and its eyes were made of two little black beads dyed from berries. The little Indian maiden loved her kachina, carried it with her when she played and slept with it in her arms at night.

When this little girl heard what the Great Spirit wanted she almost cried, for she felt in her heart that nothing among her people was more loved than her own doll. But she looked up and saw the shadows of pain in the face of her hungry mother. She saw how thin was the face of her baby brother strapped to his mother's back in his cradle. She looked down at her beloved little doll, held it tightly to her breast and slipped away to her father's wigwam where she lay for a long time with her face pressed close against her doll.

Kachina Brings the Spring
From <u>When the Storm God Rides</u> Pages 15–25

(continued)

The lodges were still and the fire in the middle of the camp had died down to red embers when the little girl came out again. In her arms was her doll. She knew she loved her kachina more than anything else was loved in the tribe, and she had decided to give it up as the Great Spirit had asked, so that her people would be happy again.

She cried a little bit as she laid twigs on the dying embers of the fire. But she blew the fire until it spring up into a blaze that made the shiny eyes of her doll sparkle, so they seemed to be bright with tears, like her own. She hugged the doll and kissed it. Now she laid it in the middle of the flames. Quickly the flames began to eat the doll. The blue feathers on its head were gone, the tiny shoes turned into smoke, the beady eyes fell off the burning face into the fire, and soon there was nothing left of the doll the little girl had loved.

Now she raked out the ashes and sat down to watch them cool. When they had cooled she took them in her two hands and held them up while the cool wind blew them out of her hands and into the darkness. Finally the little girl stooped and patted the ground where the ashes of her doll had lain. Then a wonderful thing happened. Where the ground was bare and hard before, it was now covered with soft leaves that felt warm to her cold little hands. The sharp cold of the night wind now was gone, and the smell of spring flowers seemed to fill the air around her. The Great Spirit must have been pleased with the offering of her doll. Happy once more, the little girl hurried to her wigwam and lay down to sleep.

In the morning the child was awakened with the sound of joyous cries outside. She heard drums beating and heard dancing feet. The Indians were singing. She peeped outside and saw that she had pleased the Great Spirit, because for the first time in many moons a misty rain was falling, a rain that was good to the thirsty earth. The cold wind was gone, too. The warm south wind was gently blowing through the rain and rustling trees that were heavy with new green leaves. Everywhere the hills and prairies were covered with strange and lovely flowers the Indians had never seen before. When she ran to pick one of them she saw that they were shaped like the bonnet of feathers her doll had worn, and blue like those feathers. At the heart of each small blossom was a speck of red, just like the red of the fire, which had burned her doll. And the tips of buds were silver gray, like the ashes that were left after it had burned.

When the little girl hurried with one of the new flowers to the Indians they knew what had happened. She had given her doll to the Great Spirit and he had given back to her millions of flowers that were now lying on the hills like a piece of blue sky fallen to earth. And spring had come at last. The Indians named the new flowers blue bonnets, because they were like the blue bonnet of the little girl's doll. Today, when the bluebonnets appear on the Texas prairies, it is a sign that the Great Spirit has once more returned springtime to the earth.

Activity #60: GENEROSITY
I'm a Star . . . . You're a Star

> "When you are in doubt, be still, and wait;
> when doubt no longer exists for you, then go forward
> with courage."
>
> — White Eagle

Grades: 3-5

Purpose: To teach students how courage and generosity often go together.

Materials: *Star Boy* by Paul Goble (ISBN 0-689-71499-8)
Star Template
Crayons, map pencils, markers
Pencil
Chart paper or board

Procedures:
- On the board, or chart paper, write the word "courage"
- Brainstorm with students what having courage means, and who they have known to have courage.
- Discuss how sometimes it takes courage to be generous to others.
- Read *Star Boy*.
  Discuss: • Who in this story had courage?
  • How did the chief's daughter help Star Boy have courage?
  • How was this a form of generosity?
  • How can we have courage to be generous to each other?
- Distribute Star Template.
- Students write or draw outside the star the names of people who have been courageous and generous to them.
- Students write or draw inside the star the names of people to whom the students have had the courage to be generous.
- Share when finished.

Extension:
- Display the Stars in the room.
- Journal about what having courage means, and how it feels to have courage and be generous to someone.

Courageous And Generous Stars

Activity #61: GENEROSITY
Teaching the Young

"Children were encouraged to develop strict discipline and a high regard for sharing. When a girl picked her first berries and dug her first roots, they were given away to an elder so she would share her future success. When a child carried water for the home, an elder would give compliments, pretending to taste meat in water carried by a boy or berries in that of a girl. The child was encouraged not to be lazy and to grow straight like a sapling."

— Mourning Dove Salish

Grades: 1-8

Purpose: To provide opportunity to experience the inner warmth of helping others
To develop a sense of mastery by being chosen to read to others

Materials: *Dream Wolf* by Paul Goble (ISBN 0-02-736585-9)
Various books
Paper and crayons
Teaching the Young Worksheet

Procedures:
- Read *Dream Wolf.*
  - **Discuss:**
    - How did Tiblo help his little sister Tanksi?
    - How did the wolf help the two lost children?
    - How do you think the children felt when the wolf helped them?
    - How do you think the wolf felt when he was able to help the children?
- Get permission from a Kindergarten or Pre-K class to have students come in and read to the children.
- After the students have read them a book or two, have them help the younger students to draw pictures about the books.
- When the students get back to class, have them write about how it felt to help the younger students.
- Younger students may use the Teaching the Young Worksheet.
- Discuss feelings about the activity.

Extension:
- Have the older students also draw a picture for the younger child to keep.

Teaching the Young

Today I read to _____ .

I read a book called _____ .

I think that the child felt _____
that I came to read to them today.

I felt _____
after reading to the child.

Check one:

I ☐ did ☐ did not
enjoy doing this activity.

178

Activity #62: GENEROSITY
I Offer You My Hand

> "I ran to the spring to fetch water for them when they were thirsty. By these little services I won their affection."
>
> — Playful Calf

Grades: 1-5

Purpose: To learn about the concept of unselfishness
To provide opportunity to practice unselfishness

Materials: *Legend of the Bluebonnet* by Tomie dePaola
I Offer You My Hand Worksheet

Procedures:
- Read *Legend of the Bluebonnet.*
  Discuss:
  - The unselfishness of the young girl.
  - Have the class brainstorm and list unselfish acts of love and friendship that a student can show to others in their school family.
  - Remind them the girl did this act of kindness for people who actually were not her own family members.
  - Relate this to the concept of extended family.
  - We are all family.
  - We are all interconnected.
  - Mother Earth is the mother of all beings.
- Have students fill out the I Offer You My Hand Worksheet, listing "extended family" to whom they can extend the hand of caring.

Extension:
- Contract with students to literally extend their hand to a specific person during the week.

I Offer You My Hand

Below are people to whom I can extend my hand of Generosity.

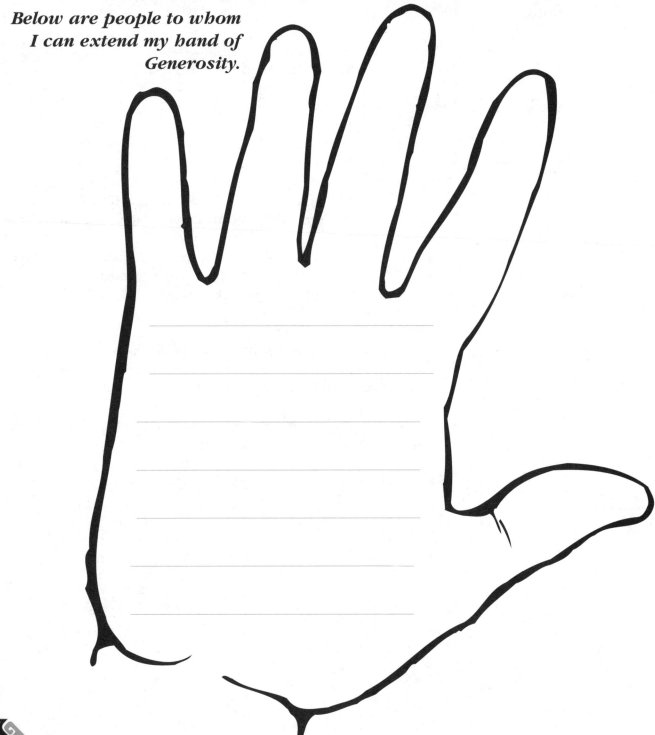

Activity #63: GENEROSITY
Brothers and Sisters

> "All things are connected.
> Whatever befalls the earth befalls the sons of the earth.
> Man did not weave the web of life. He is merely a strand in it.
> Whatever he does to the web, he does to himself."
>
> — Chief Seattle (1854)

Grades: K-8

Purpose: To teach the importance of caring for the earth and our country
                   To teach the interconnectedness of all living things
                   To extend the concept of generosity to caring for the earth
                   To promote a personal sense of commitment to the earth

Materials: *Brother Eagle, Sister Sky* by Seattle and Susan Jeffers (ISBN 0803709692)
                   Brother Eagle, Sister Sky Worksheets
                   Markers or colored pencils

Procedures: • Read *Brother Eagle, Sister Sky.*
        Discuss: • The importance of caring for the earth and our country.
                • Emphasize how we are all connected as part of the web of life.
                • What we do to each other we do to ourselves.
                • So, how do we want to treat ourselves?
                   • Have the students complete the Brother Eagle, Sister Sky Worksheet.
                   • Older students will write their answers on the worksheet with lines.
                   • Younger students will draw one thing in Nature to which they are attracted
                     and for which they would like to care.

Extension: • Have students take the worksheet home to discuss with family.
                   • Give them a blank worksheet to be filled out by the family.
                   • Bring the family worksheet to the next session to be discussed.

Brother Eagle, Sister Sky

List the parts of Nature to which you feel particularly attracted.
Next to each item, write what you can do to care for that part of nature.

Brother Eagle,
Sister Sky

This is a drawing of a part of Nature that I really like.

Name _____

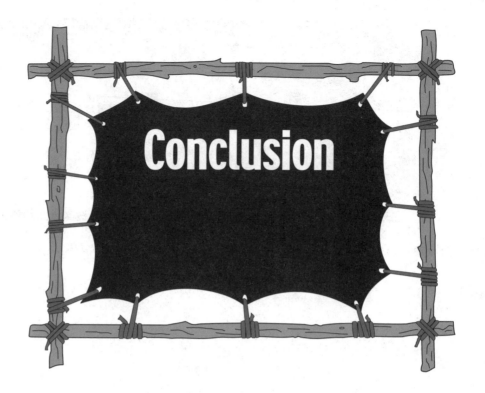

Conclusion

The innate human need for connection is not only an emotional and social need, but a need which is also deeply rooted neurologically in the human brain. The ancient wisdom of the Native American traditions can be used as a vehicle for the modern-day group counselor to assist in the healing of children who feel disconnected from society, themselves, and nature. The harmony inherent in the Native American philosophy can be a group-counseling vehicle to help heal the disconnectedness that children feel and are acting out. This group experience of interrelatedness has the potential to assist children in reconnecting to society and to aid in the reconnection of their fragmented selves. The use of pet therapy and nature therapy are natural adjuncts to the use of Native American philosophy and activities. The use of animals and nature activities within the group process are ways to make concrete the Native American wisdom, which teaches the interconnected condition of all beings.

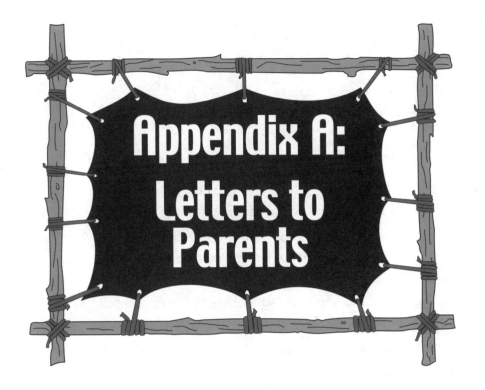

Appendix A: Letters to Parents

- Belonging Letter to Parents

- Mastery Letter to Parents

- Independence Letter to Parents

- Generosity Letter to Parents

Dear Parent/Guardian,

Your child, _____, has been invited to participate in a counseling group targeted for students who are having difficulty with compliance, cooperation and respect. This group is designed to use Native American wisdom to help reinforce the harmonious coexistence of everything in our natural environment.

By using this approach, we hope to increase your child's self-esteem, self-confidence, self-concept and pride by providing a different way of thinking and behaving to allow him/her to connect with others, community, nature and a universal spirit of compassion.

One of the basic principles regarding this approach is focusing on the student's need for belonging. Students must feel that they belong to some sort of group. If this need is not met, they can become alienated and act out their sense of disconnectedness. However, when this basic need is met, students become cooperative, friendly, affectionate, respectful, trusting and sympathetic. This need for belonging can be corrected through relationships of trust and intimacy. This counseling approach uses Native American wisdom to guide the student in his/her efforts to connect in positive ways.

The group will begin on _____.

Please sign below to signify your permission for your son/daughter to participate in this group experience.

_____   _____
Parent's Signature   Date

Dear Parent/Guardian,

Your child, _____, has been invited to participate in a counseling group targeted for students who are having difficulty with compliance, cooperation and respect. This group is designed to use Native American wisdom to help reinforce the harmonious coexistence of everything in our natural environment.

By using this approach, we hope to increase your child's self-esteem, self-confidence, self-concept and pride by providing a different way of thinking and behaving to allow him/her to connect with others, community, nature and a universal spirit or compassion.

One of the basic principles regarding this approach is focusing on the student's need for mastery. Students have an innate need to interact competently with others. If this need is not met, they can become alienated and act out their sense of disconnectedness because they feel that someone with more competence is a rival instead of a resource. However, when students experience mastery, they are able to understand that achievement is sought for personal reasons, not out of competition. This need for mastery can be met by building self-esteem and confidence. This counseling approach will use Native American wisdom to guide the student as he/she strives to build self-esteem and confidence.

The group will begin on _____.

Please sign below to signify your permission for your son/daughter to participate in this group experience.

_____   _____

Parent's Signature   Date

Dear Parent/Guardian,

Your child, _____, has been invited to participate in a counseling group for students who are having trouble with compliance, cooperation and respect. This group is designed to use Native American wisdom to help reinforce the harmonious coexistence of everything in our natural environment.

By using this approach, we hope to increase your child's self-esteem, self-confidence, self-concept and pride by providing a different way of thinking and behaving to allow him/her to connect with others, community, nature and a universal spirit of compassion.

One of the basic principles regarding this approach is focusing on the student's need for independence. When this need is unmet, students typically exhibit a sense of emotional disconnectedness and often lack proper empathy. Meeting the need of generosity will instill a joy of helping others by providing students with a sense of power and purpose by contributing to others' lives.

The group will begin on _____.

Please sign below to signify your permission for your son/daughter to participate in this group experience.

_____   _____
Parent's Signature   Date

Dear Parent/Guardian,

Your child, _____, has been invited to participate in a counseling group for students who are having trouble with compliance, cooperation and respect. This group is designed to use Native American wisdom to help reinforce the harmonious coexistence of everything in our natural environment.

By using this approach, we hope to increase your child's self-esteem, self-confidence, self-concept and pride by providing a different way of thinking and behaving to allow him/her to connect with others, community, nature and a universal spirit of compassion.

One of the basic principles regarding this approach is focusing on the student's need for generosity. When this need is unmet, students typically exhibit a sense of emotional disconnectedness and often lack proper empathy. Meeting the need of generosity will instill a joy of helping others by providing students with a sense of power and purpose by contributing to others' lives.

The group will begin on _____.

Please sign below to signify your permission for your son/daughter to participate in this group experience.

_____   _____

Parent's Signature   Date

Appendix B: Contract Forms

- Belonging Contract

- Mastery Contract

- Independence Contract

- Generosity Contract

Belonging

I, _____,

agree to work on the following behavior in an effort to

develop my ability to experience a greater sense of

Belonging.

_____

_____

_____

_____

_____   _____

Signature   Date

_____   _____

Witness   Date

CONTRACT
Mastery

I,_____,

agree to the following behavior in order to

develop an increased sense of mastery.

_____

_____

_____

_____

_____

_____   _____
Signature   Date

_____   _____
Witness   Date

CONTRACT
Independence

I,_____,

agree to the following behavior in order to

develop increased independence.

_____

_____

_____

_____

_____

_____   _____
Signature   Date

_____   _____
Witness   Date

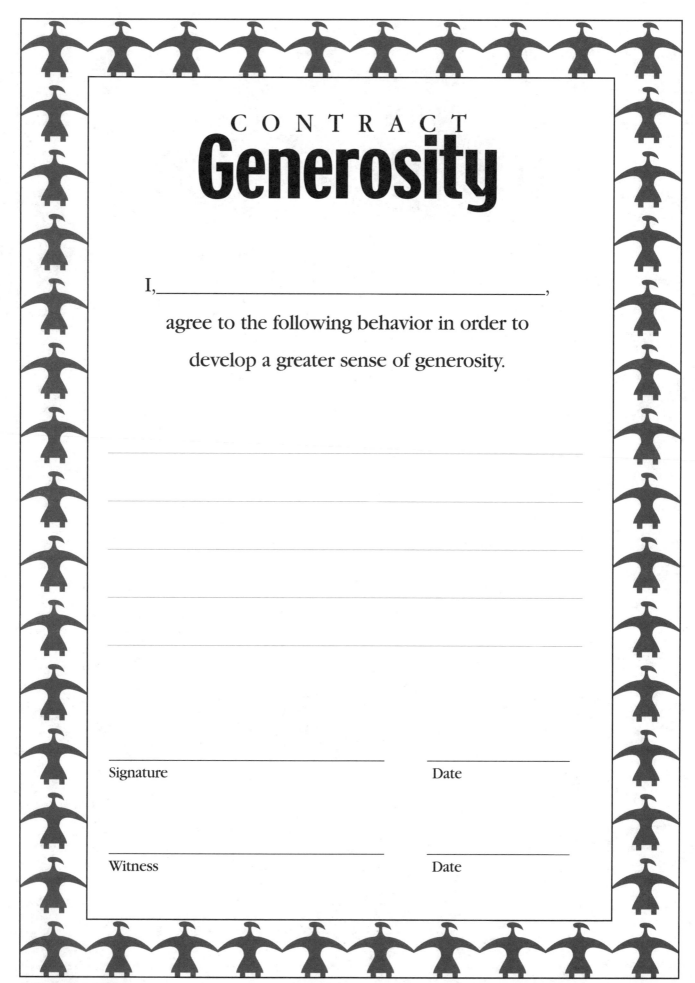

CONTRACT

Generosity

I,_____,

agree to the following behavior in order to

develop a greater sense of generosity.

_____

_____

_____

_____

_____

_____   _____
Signature   Date

_____   _____
Witness   Date

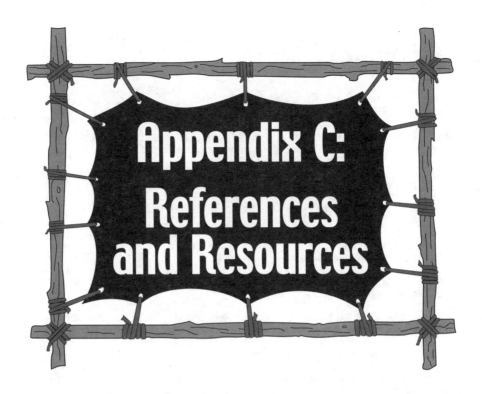

Appendix C: References and Resources

Ascione, F. R. (1992). Enhancing children's attitudes about the humane treatment of animals: generalization to human-directed empathy. *Anthrozoos*, 5(3), 176-191.

Axelson, J.A. (1999). *Counseling and development in a multicultural society (3rd ed.)*. Pacific Grove, CA: Brooks/Cole.

Beck, A. & Katcher, A. H. (1984). A new look at pet-facilitated therapy. *Journal of the American Veterinary Medical Association*, 184 (4), 414-421.

Bergeson, F. J. (1989). *The effects of pet facilitated therapy on the self-esteem and socialization of primary school children*. Paper presented at the 5th International Conference on the Relationship between Humans and Animals, Monaco.

Blue, G. F. (1986). The value of pets in children's lives. *Childhood Education*, 63, 85-90.

Brendtro, L. K., Brokenleg, M., & Van Bockern, S. (2002). *Reclaiming youth at risk: Our hope for the future*. Bloomington, IN: National Education Service.

Brendtro, L. K., Brokenleg, M., & Van Bockern, S. (1991). The circle of courage. *Beyond Behavior, 2(1), 5-12*.

Brendtro, L. K., & Van Bockern, S. (1998). Courage for the discouraged: A psychoeducational approach to troubled and troubling children. In R. J. Whelan (Ed.), *Emotional and behavioral disorders: A 25 year focus* (pp. 229-252). Denver, CO: Love.

Brinson, J.A., & Lee, C. C. (1997). Culturally-responsive group leadership: An integrative model for experienced practitioners. In H. Forester-Miller & J.A. Kottler (Eds.) *Issues and challenges for group practitioners* (pp. 43-56). Denver, CO: Love.

Brokenleg, M. (1996). Unshackled by visions and values. *Reclaiming Children and Youth*, 5, 136-139.

Bryant, B. K. (1985). The neighborhood walk. A study of sources of support in middle childhood from the child's perspective. *Monographs of the Society for Research in Child Development*, 50 (serial no. 210).

Bryant, B. K. (1986). *The relevance of family and neighborhood animals to social emotional development in middle childhood*. Davis, CA: University of California, Davis.

Carr, T. (2004). *Return to the land: A search for compassion*. Chapin, SC: Youthlight, Inc.

REFERENCES *(continued)*

Covert, A. M., Whiren, A. P., Keith, J. & Nelson, D. (1985). Pets, early adolescents and families. *Marriage and Family Review, 8,* 95-108.

Crompton, J. & Sellar, C. (1981, Summer). Do outdoor education experiences contribute to positive development in the affective domain? *Journal of Environmental Education, 12(4),* 21-21.

Cullinan, D. (2002). *Students with emotional and behavior disorders: An introduction for teachers and other helping professionals.* Columbus, OH: Merrill Prentice Hall.

Cusack, O. (1987). *Pets and mental health.* New York: Haworth Press.

Davis, J. H. (1986). Children and pets: A therapeutic connection, *The Latham Letter, 7(4).*

Deloria, V., Jr. (1994). *God is red: A Native view of religion.* Golden, DO: Fulcrum.

Dufrene, P. M. (1990). Exploring Native American symbolism. *Journal of Multicultural and Cross-Cultural Research in Art Education, 8,* 38-50.

Eisenberger, N. I. & Lieberman, M. D. (2004). Why rejection hurts: A common neural alarm system for physical and social pain. *Trends in Cognitive Sciences. 8(7),* 294-300. UCLA.

Fogle, B. (1981). *Interrelations between people and pets.* Springfield, IL: Charles C. Thomas.

Furr, S. R. (2000). Structuring the group experience: A format for designing psychoeducational groups. *Journal for Specialists in Group Work, 25,* 29-49.

Garrett, M.T. & Crutchfield, L. B. (1997). Moving full circle: A unity model of group work with children. *The Journal for Specialists in Group Work, 22(3),* 175-188.

Garrett, M.T., Garrett, J.T., & Brotherton, D. (2001). Inner circle/outer circle: A group technique based on Native American healing circles. *The Journal for Specialists in Group Work, 26(1),* 17-30.

Gladding, S.T. (1999). *Group work: A counseling specialty* (2nd ed.). Columbus, OH: Merrill.

Haley-Banez, L., & Walden, S. L. (1999). Diversity in group work: Using optimal theory to understand group process and dynamics. *Journal for Specialists in Group Work, 24,* 404-422.

Hirschfelder, A., & Kreipe de Montano, M. (1993). *The Native American almanac: A portrait of Native America today.* New York: Macmillan.

Kaplan, R. (1992). *The psychological benefits of nearby nature: The role of horticulture in human well-being and social development.* A national symposium. Portland, OR: Timber Press.

Kaufmann, M. (Ed.). (1999). *Growing up humane in a violent world: An agenda for a non-violent future.* Englewood, CO: American Humane Association.

Kellert, S.R. & Wilson, E.O. (Eds). (1993). *Biophilia hypothesis.* Washington DC-Covelo, CA: Island Press/Shearwater Books.

Melson, G. F. (1990). *Fostering inter-connectedness with animals and nature: The developmental benefits for children.* [On-line]. Available: http://info@deltasociety.org.

Melson, G. F., & Peet, S. H. (1988). *Attachment to pets, empathy and self-concept in young children.* Paper presented to the annual meeting of the Delta Society, Orlando, FL.

Nebbe, L. L. (1995). *Nature as a guide: Nature in counseling, therapy, and education.* (2nd ed.). Minneapolis, MN: Educational Media Corporation.

Oswalt, W. H., & Neely, S. (1999). *This land was theirs: A study of North American Indians* (6th ed.) Mountain View, CA: Mayfield.

Paul, E. S. (1992). *Pets in childhood, individual variation in childhood pet ownership.* Doctoral thesis, University of Cambridge, England.

Reyhner, J. (Ed.). (1992). *Teaching American Indian students.* Norman: University of Oklahoma Press.

Stratton, F. (1936). *When the storm god rides.* Dallas: Charles Scribner's Sons.